Historical Atlases of South Asia,
Central Asia, and the Middle East

A HISTORICAL ATLAS OF
SAUDI ARABIA

Nancy L. Stair

The Rosen Publishing Group, Inc.

To Nick and Jen

Published in 2003 by The Rosen Publishing Group, Inc.
29 East 21st Street, New York, NY 10010

Copyright © 2003 by The Rosen Publishing Group, Inc.

First Edition

All rights reserved. No part of this book may be reproduced in any form without permission in writing from the publisher, except by a reviewer.

Library of Congress Cataloging-in-Publication Data

Stair, Nancy L.
 A Historical Atlas of Saudi Arabia / Nancy L. Stair.—1st ed.
 p. cm.—(Historical atlases of South Asia, Central Asia and the Middle East)
 Summary: Maps and text chronicle the history of this Middle Eastern country that leads the world in oil production.
 Includes bibliographical references and index.
 ISBN: 978-1-4358-9087-9
 1. Saudi Arabia—History—Maps for children. 2. Saudi Arabia—Maps for children.
 [1. Saudi Arabia—History. 2. Atlases.]
 I. Title. II. Series.

G2249.31.S1 S8 2002
912.538—dc21

2002031030 2002031755

Manufactured in the United States of America

Cover image: Maps of Saudi Arabia from the seventeenth century *(background)* and present day *(center)*. Saudi Arabia's present crown prince, Abdullah *(top left)*. Sixteenth-century Arabic illustration of the Koran *(bottom left)*, Islam's holy book. An eighteenth-century Indian portrait of the caliph Uthman *(bottom right)*.

Contents

	Introduction	5
1.	Mapping the Land	7
2.	Ancient Arabia	13
3.	Early Tribes	17
4.	Power Struggles	22
5.	The Rise of Islam	29
6.	Arabia After Muhammad	36
7.	The Wahhabis and the House of Sa'ud	42
8.	Modern Saudi Arabia	52
	Timeline	60
	Glossary	61
	For More Information	62
	For Further Reading	62
	Bibliography	62
	Index	63

INTRODUCTION

Although Saudi Arabia is often portrayed as a country of repression, it is also one that has a rich and vibrant history. A land of extremes, today Saudi Arabia remains a nation undergoing change even though it is now considered a modern, industrialized society made rich from its supply of oil reserves. Despite its progress, however, many of its citizens remain nomads constantly in search of an adequate water supply.

Saudi Arabia is a country of vast deserts, though it is largely surrounded by water. In the northeast, the Persian Gulf borders the land. Saudi Arabia's southern border is bound by three countries east to west—the United Arab Emirates, Oman, and the Republic of Yemen. Separating Saudi Arabia from Africa is the Red Sea. The country's

Saudi Arabia, as it is known today, became a unified nation because of the campaigns of Abd al-Aziz ibn Sa'ud. By 1932, Abd al-Aziz proclaimed the country the Kingdom of Saudi Arabia, and in 1936, commercial amounts of oil were discovered within its soil, infusing its economy with foreign money and completely changing the lives of its citizens. Within the span of eight years following the discovery, four American companies joined to form Aramco, the Arabian American Oil Company. By the 1990s, Iraq's invasion of Kuwait and the Gulf War between the United States and Iraq that followed each had a great effect on Saudi Arabia.

The Muslims pictured here are practicing one of the five pillars of Islam—to pray at least five times per day facing the Ka'aba (also spelled Kaaba or Ka'bah), the center of the Great Mosque in the city of Mecca. When praying, Muslims are commonly required to kneel with their foreheads touching the floor while barefoot.

northern boundary extends almost 870 miles (1,400 kilometers) from the Gulf of Aqaba in the west to Ras al Khafji on the Persian Gulf. Its northern section is completely covered by desert.

Saudi Arabia is also an ancient land of religion. Besides being known for its abundant natural resources, the country is famous for its holy cities, Mecca and Medina. Every year, Muslims (followers of the Islamic religion) from all over the world travel thousands of miles to Mecca in order to make a pilgrimage, or hajj, to honor their sole deity, Allah. And each day, Muslims around the world kneel and pray toward Mecca, where thousands of years ago the prophet Muhammad spread Islam.

Saudi citizens are entirely Muslim. They live by the laws of Islam, or the Sharia, and expect their government, considered an absolute monarchy, to abide by those same strict principles. It is a county without legislature or political parties. Because of these strict religious laws, outsiders sometimes view Saudi Arabia as a nation of absolutes. Women cannot work outside the home or even drive a car. A person's heritage dictates how he or she will marry, work, and live. There are few countries in the world that differ from the United States and Canada as much as Saudi Arabia does. Reading this book, however, will help you understand this mysterious land and its ancient roots.

1 MAPPING THE LAND

Situated in West Asia, just east of Africa, Saudi Arabia is the largest country on the Arabian Peninsula, occupying approximately 80 percent of the area. It is slightly more than one-fifth the size of the United States. Its capital and largest city is Riyadh.

The Red Sea borders the country on its western coast, separating it from Egypt, the Sudan, Eritrea, and Ethiopia. The Red Sea forms a coastal border of almost 1,118 miles (1,800 kilometers) that extends south to the Republic of Yemen along a mountain ridge.

The Regions of Saudi Arabia

Saudi Arabia is divided into four regions. The first is the central region, in the heart of the country; the second is the western region, which lies along the Red Sea coast. The third, or southern region, contains the Red Sea–Yemen border area. The final, or eastern, region contains the deserts rich in natural oil deposits.

The Najd, or the central region, is a vast eroded plateau that is considered the heartland of Saudi Arabia. It consists of highlands, broad valleys, dry

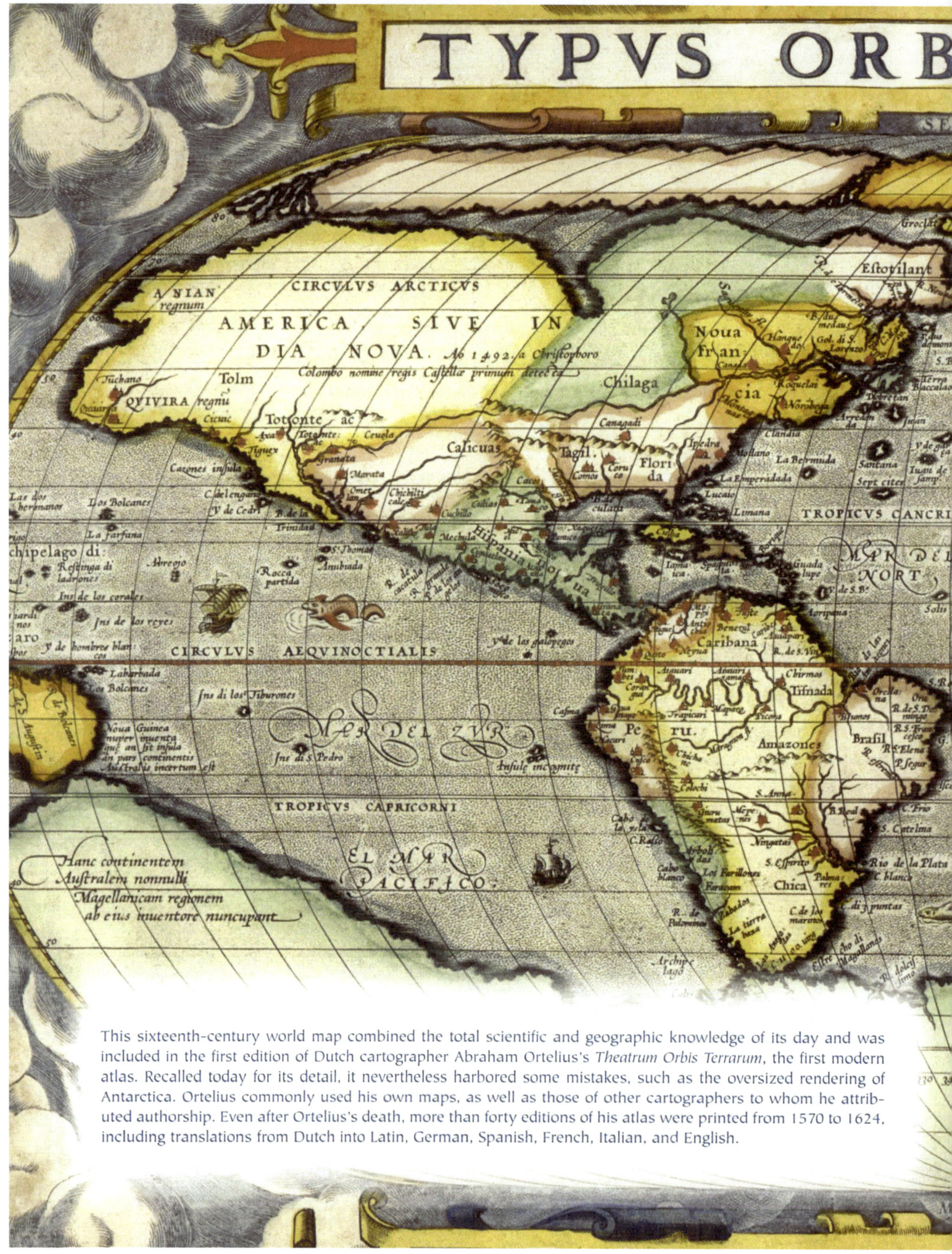

This sixteenth-century world map combined the total scientific and geographic knowledge of its day and was included in the first edition of Dutch cartographer Abraham Ortelius's *Theatrum Orbis Terrarum*, the first modern atlas. Recalled today for its detail, it nevertheless harbored some mistakes, such as the oversized rendering of Antarctica. Ortelius commonly used his own maps, as well as those of other cartographers to whom he attributed authorship. Even after Ortelius's death, more than forty editions of his atlas were printed from 1570 to 1624, including translations from Dutch into Latin, German, Spanish, French, Italian, and English.

riverbeds, and wet marshlands thought to be the remains of ancient seas. Most of the central region is arid, or dry desert, with some oases, or fertile places, in the north. Riyadh, the present Saudi capital and fastest-growing city, is also located in the Najd.

East of the mountainous barrier, which defined ancient trade routes, the Najd is the traditional home of the ruling Sa'ud family. It was also home to the Shammar tribes, which were the harshest foes of the Al Sa'ud beginning in the late nineteenth century.

Hijaz, or the western region, lies in the range of mountains that run parallel to the Red Sea coast. Hijaz is home to the greatest variety of people in the country, ranging from desert-dwelling Arabs to African descendants.

Hijaz has two zones, a narrow coastal plain and a mountainous area. The mountains contain wadis, which are dried streams that sometimes fill with runoff water during

Black Gold in the Desert

Al Hasa, Saudi Arabia's eastern region, contains massive petroleum resources, making the kingdom the world's top producer of oil. Oil was discovered there in 1936 by the U.S.-owned Arabian Standard Oil Company, which later became the Arabian American Oil Company (Aramco). Commercial production began in 1938, leading to an oil boom and improvements in transportation throughout the kingdom, including the construction of the Al-Dammam-Riyadh railroad and the Al-Dammam port. Saudi Arabia's proven reserves are estimated at more than 260 billion barrels, or about one-quarter of the world's total oil reserves. Oil accounts for 75 percent of the country's budget revenues and 90 percent of its export earnings.

The riders pictured in this photo are taking what is known as a seismic oil survey, that is, they are searching for oil in the deserts of Saudi Arabia by recording vibrations in the earth. Seismographs record reflected sound waves and provide insight into what might lie below the earth's surface.

Muslim pilgrims pray around the holy Ka'aba in Mecca in February 2001. At least one million foreigners arrive in Saudi Arabia for the annual pilgrimage to Islam's holiest sites in Mecca. Muslims believe that the prophet Abraham, like Muhammad, was a messenger of God and that his son Ishmael built the first structure in the city. The hajj, or pilgrimage to Mecca, is one of the five pillars of Islam that each Muslim is required to make at least once in his or her lifetime if he or she is healthy and has adequate resources.

the rainy season. Hijaz contains the holiest cities of Islam, Mecca and Medina, which are visited by some two million devout Muslims each year. The busy seaport of Jeddah, a thriving commercial center, is also located there.

Asir, or Saudi Arabia's southern region, is a fertile area of coastal mountains in the southwest bordering the Republic of Yemen. Mountain peaks in this region rise 10,521 feet (3,207 meters) and adequate rainfall supports a variety of natural vegetation in this densely populated area.

Finally, Saudi Arabia's eastern region, Al Ahsa or Al Hasa, was named after its great oasis. Al Hasa, a fertile area, contains lush green gardens that farmers tended in the middle of the desert. This is where most Saudi oil is found, and it is home to the oil cities of Dhahran and Damman.

Northern Saudi Arabia, or the area north of an-Nafud, is considered a

The Great Deserts

The entire southern region of Saudi Arabia is home to the Ar Rab' al-Khali, or the Empty Quarter. A desert that covers more than one third of the country—approximately 264,000 square miles (424,866 kilometers)—Ar Rab' al-Khali is uninhabited because of its extreme temperatures. Some of its desert sands extend to the Gulf of Oman in the southeast and the Republic of Yemen in the southwest. Sand dunes in this desolate region are shifted by winds that push the terrain into hills reaching more than 150 feet (46 meters) in height.

The Great Desert, or an-Nafud, a smaller arid area, covers approximately 22,000 square miles (45.7 sq km) and is located in the north-central section of the Arabian Peninsula. It is home to cultivated sections, and winter rains sometimes give rise to grasses that permit nomadic herding during the spring.

This satellite image of the Arabian Peninsula offers a glimpse of Saudi Arabia as a paradox—a country nearly surrounded by water, yet one mostly covered by desert. The Empty Quarter sometimes provides a home to bedouins, nomadic wanderers who camp close to desert wells where camels drink brackish water unfit for human consumption. Instead of surviving on water, the bedouins drink fresh camel's milk. Never a home of permanent-dwelling Arabs, the Empty Quarter is sometimes a dangerous expanse of sand, many times blown by harsh winds that can sting anyone who has exposed skin. Years before the Empty Quarter was traveled, foreign cartographers optimistically—yet mistakenly—added lakes, rivers, and even towns to the barren desert region.

part of the Syrian Desert. The land, known as Badiyat ash Sham, is covered with grass and scrub vegetation and is used for pastureland by nomadic herders. For thousands of years, caravan routes between the Mediterranean Sea and the central and southern peninsula passed through this area.

2 ANCIENT ARABIA

During ancient times, hunter-gatherers migrated from Africa to the Arabian Peninsula, which was then lush and fertile. About 15,000 years ago, the weather there grew warmer and the deserts expanded. As a result, the harsh climate of the peninsula made Arabia's interior regions difficult to access. Except for coastal areas and a few major settlements and oases, this harsh climate prevented development. Arabia could produce agriculture to support only a small population.

Archaeologists have discovered rock drawings in Arabia's desert in which hunters and herders of the period depicted their daily lives. Scholars believe that they became nomadic after being pushed from their settlements by expanding tribes.

Nearly one-fourth of the region's earliest inhabitants were nomadic tribes, known as bedouins, who were forced to search for water. In time, they began to herd camels, goats, and sheep. Since the region had no permanent lakes or streams, bedouins had to continuously search for oases from which their animals could drink. Others settled in small villages along the coasts and began farming and trading.

Trade Routes

Wedged between three major continents—Africa, Europe, and Asia—the Arabian Peninsula was a vital

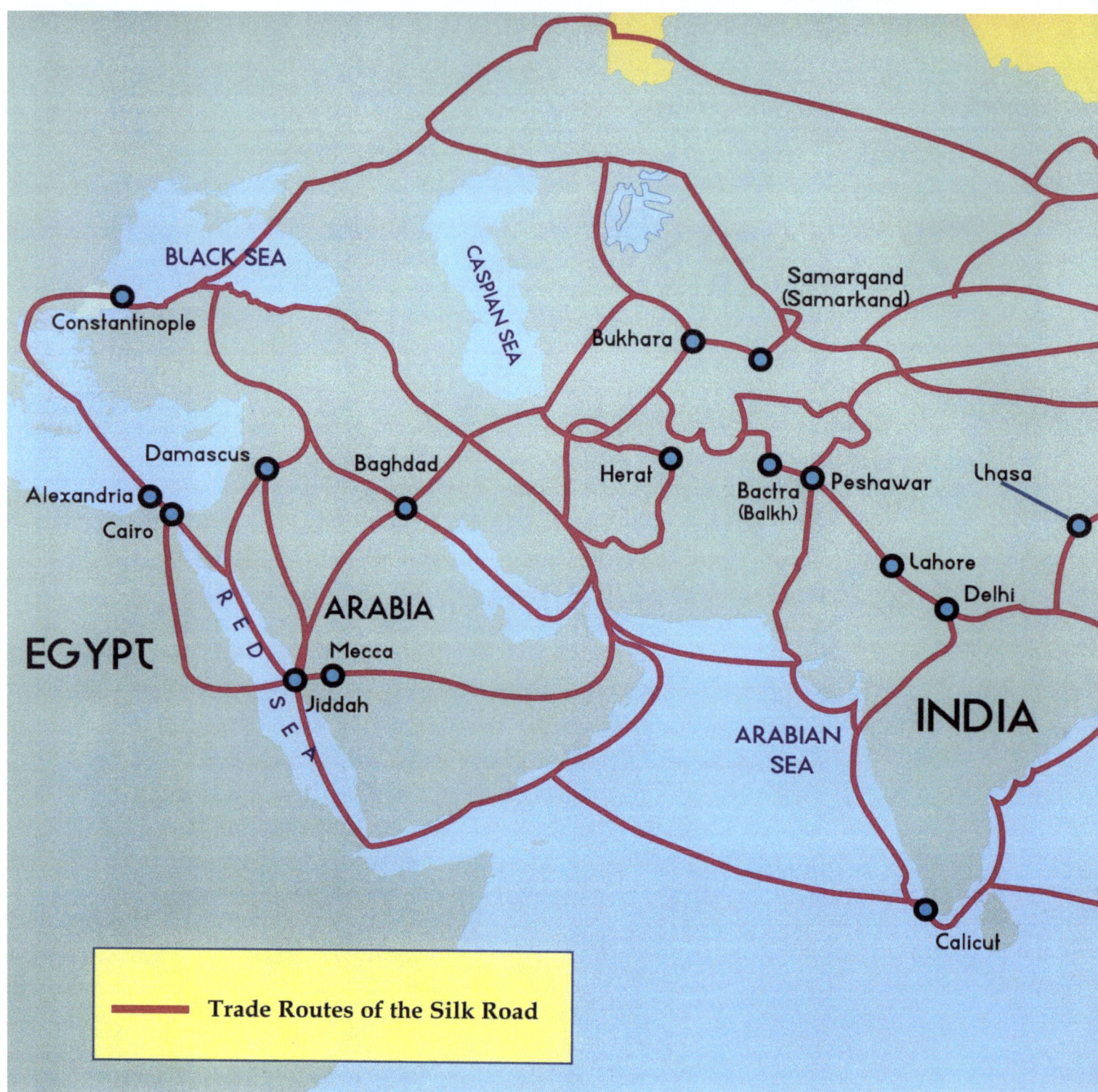

Trade Routes of the Silk Road

Arabs were using the trade routes of the Silk Road as early as 900 BC, though the routes themselves developed much earlier, first along the Fertile Crescent of Mesopotamia. The Silk Road's name, which is suggestive of one road, is actually inaccurate. The Silk Road is a 5,000-mile (8,047-km) link of ancient routes over land and water. Some routes were well developed and safe from bandits, while others were less protected. Few traders actually made the entire transcontinental journey along the route, though the goods traveled from one side of Asia to the other. And though it might have been named for the exquisite silks that found their way across Asia to Europe, many other luxury items were carried by caravan along the route, including precious metals and stones (such as jade, bronze, and iron), ivory, glass, ceramics, and gun powder.

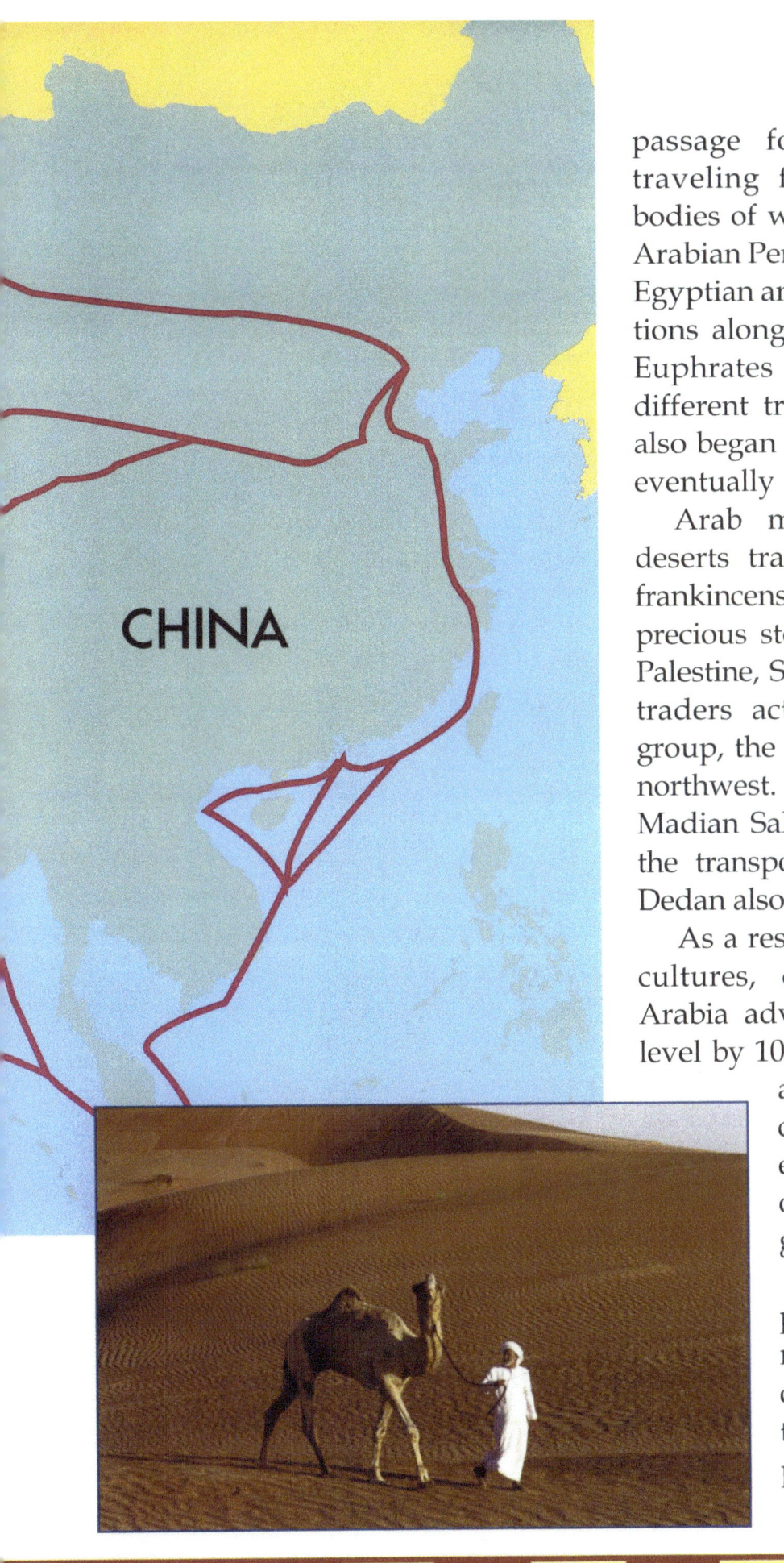

passage for caravans of traders traveling from east to west. The bodies of water on either side of the Arabian Peninsula made neighboring Egyptian and Mesopotamian civilizations along the Nile and the Tigris-Euphrates Rivers accessible. Once different tribes communicated, they also began trading with one another, eventually gaining wealth.

Arab merchants traveled over deserts transporting items such as frankincense, myrrh, silk, spices, gold, precious stones, and ivory to Egypt, Palestine, Syria, and Babylonia. Local traders acted as middlemen. One group, the Nabataeans, settled in the northwest. They built a stronghold at Madian Salih to enforce their role in the transport of goods. The city of Dedan also did a brisk spice trade.

As a result of the contact between cultures, civilization in southern Arabia advanced to a sophisticated level by 1000 BC. Arab life improved after a method for saddling camels was developed that enabled the transportation of larger loads across greater distances.

Trans-Arabian trade produced two important results. One was the rise of cities that could help maintain caravans. The most prosperous villages were

Desert Heat

The Arabian Peninsula is one of the few places in the world where summer temperatures rise above 120° F (48° C). The 750-mile (1,207-kilometer) landmass has a long, dry summer and a short, cool winter, when slight rain falls. Annual rainfall in Riyadh averages 4 inches (100 millimeters) and falls only between January and May. Because of the dry climate, the entire country has no permanent rivers, lakes, or streams.

Some areas of Saudi Arabia do not see rain for as long as ten years at a stretch. When rain does fall, it fills dry gulches. Torrents of water fill the wadis during the brief periods of rain, yet they remain dry for the rest of the year. Saudi Arabia is so dry, in fact, that less than one percent of its total land is suitable for cultivation.

Since it lacks cloud cover, has high temperatures, and gets little rain, heat escapes from the deserts at night, and temperatures drop rapidly. These temperature swings produce strong winds. The wind that blows from the north in early summer is called the *shamaal*, meaning "northerly wind." The *kaus*, or "southerly wind," blows from the southeast and comes less frequently.

---

close to Mediterranean markets, but after trade developed further, smaller cities were also established. The most important of these cities was Mecca, which also owed its prosperity to its shrines.

The second result of increased trade was the contact it gave Arabs with the outside world. In the Near East, centuries before Islam, the Persians and the Romans sometimes found bordering Arab tribes drawn into their political affairs. After AD 400, both empires paid Arab tribes not only to protect their territory but also to disturb the borders of their rivals. Infighting among the tribes, however, eventually caused trade to decline. Later, portions of Arabia fell into Abyssinian and Roman rule.

3 EARLY TRIBES

Before the birth of Muhammad in AD 570 and the subsequent rise of Islam, the Arabian Peninsula was inhabited by four major tribes—the Sabaeans, the Minaeans, the Qatabanians, and the Hadramites. These tribes migrated from the Arab-Persian Gulf region in the northeast.

The four tribes erected capitals that were located in a cluster on the western, southern, and eastern fringes of a desert known to medieval Arab geographers as the Sayhad, present-day Ramlat As-Sab'atayn. This kept them near trade routes by which goods were transported up the western coast of Arabia to Gaza and finally across the peninsula to the eastern coast.

The Sabaeans

The earliest kingdom in Arabia was the Saba, or Sheba, which existed from 950 to 115 BC. It covered an area on the edge of the desert in the dry delta of the Wadi Adana. The Sabaean Empire eventually extended from Nagran to the Indian Ocean. Sabaean inscriptions show that they extended their territory by establishing colonies across the Red Sea in Abyssinia (Ethiopia).

During the biannual periods of rain, the Sabaeans were able to irrigate and cultivate the land in this otherwise rainless, arid zone. Toward the end of the

A Historical Atlas of Saudi Arabia

The Sabaeans left behind some of the earliest known written records, such as this inscription on a stone tablet. The Sabaean script probably originated in the fourth century BC. Its alphabet consisted of twenty-eight letters, and it was read from right to left. This stone tablet was found in the Republic of Yemen.

sixth century BC, two successive rulers built the Great Dam of Ma'rib.

Ma'rib was an important route that ran from land points near the Indian Ocean to the Mediterranean Sea. Other trade routes of the time followed a chain of watering places on the edge of the wadis between the mountains and the desert. Caravan routes were first mentioned in the Bible. One such story explains the visit of the legendary Queen of Sheba (Saba) to King Solomon along the frankincense route.

The last two significant leaders of the Sabaean dynasty were the kings Iisarah Yahdib and Ya'zil Bayyin, who together ruled the empire. They

The Great Dam at Ma'rib

The Ma'rib Dam was built to regulate the waters of the Wadi Sadd, also called Wadi Saba. The ancient dam, 50 feet (15 meters) high and nearly 1,800 feet (550 meters) long, was built of stone and masonry. Flanked by locks and spillways to control the flow of water, the dam fed a system of irrigation canals for more than 1,000 years. Its purpose was to irrigate 4,000 acres (1,600 hectares), supporting an agricultural region dependent on water. Successive generations of Sabaean and Himyarite rulers further improved the works, before their natural destruction in the seventh century AD.

The Great Dam of Ma'rib was located in the ancient town of Ma'rib, once a central trading center of the pre-Islamic state of Saba (950–115 BC). Called the "Paris of the Ancient World," Ma'rib is home to ancient structures such as the ruins seen in this photo, which probably date back as far as the seventh century AD.

conquered the king of the Himyarites in AD 248 or 249. Scholars know of their military operations from the inscriptions found in the Awam Temple near Ma'rib. Just decades later, the Sabaean dynasty ended.

The Minaeans

Scholars have found references to the Minaean kingdom in early Sabaean texts. The kingdom was founded on trade route monopolies and lasted from the fourth to the second century BC. Scholars believe that the Minaeans were associated with the Amir people to the north of the Minaean capital of Qarnaw (Ma'in).

The Minaeans built a second town surrounded by huge walls at Yathill, a short distance south of the capital. They established trading centers at Dedan, Qatabanian, and Hadramite. Sabaean texts also reveal an interruption of trade caused by disputes between Egyptians and the Seleucids of Syria.

The heart of the Minaean territory was the large river oasis that once extended northwest of Ma'rib, later known as al-Gawf. The Minaeans gradually became independent.

For more than a century, the Minaean Empire controlled most of the trade routes between southern Arabia and the Mediterranean Sea, a journey that could last more than two months. To protect this route, the Minaeans established a colony in the northwest. An ancient inscription describes a confrontation between the Sabaeans and Minaeans for control of trade routes. According to this writing, the two leaders of the Minaean community expressed gratitude that their property had been saved from attack by Sabaeans.

The Minaean presence in the region is reflected in their inscriptions, which refer to Gaza, Egypt, Ionia, Sidon in Phoenicia, Ammon, Moab, and Yathrib, among other ancient cities. In an epitaph on a sarcophagus found in Egypt, for example, a Minaean scribe recounted that he delivered perfumes to an Egyptian temple. On the Greek island of Delos, two Minaeans erected an altar to their native god, Wadd, and later, in the Roman world, people spoke of "Minaean frankincense" because it was mainly the Minaeans who traded this product.

The Qatabanians

The earliest references to the Qatabanians also come from Sabaean inscriptions. Around 400 BC, the Qatabanians also freed themselves from the Sabaeans and expanded their territory. At the height of its power in the third century BC, the Qataban tribe extended as far as

the Indian Ocean in the south and to the Sabaean capital of Ma'rib in the north. As these other ancient kingdoms of Arabia grew stronger, it became urgent for the Sabaeans to fortify Ma'rib. They also managed to control trade routes leading into the present-day Yemenite highlands. An inscription in the Awam Temple, dating to the fourth century BC, indicates that the Sabaeans repelled an attack by Qataban and brought peace to Ma'rib.

The heartland of the Qataban people was Wadi Bayhan. The capital, Timna, was at its northern end,

Early Tribes

and was later destroyed by the Hadramites. Other parts of Qataban fell to the Sabaeans.

The Hadramites

Fewer records remain of the Hadramite tribe than of the Sabaean, Minaean, or Qatabanian tribes. The ancient Hadramite capital of Shabwah existed on the eastern fringe of the Sayhad sands, where archaeologists have found the ruins of a large walled town, complete with a palace and temple. The main port of Hadhramaut was at Cane on the Bay of Bi'r 'Ali.

Because of the climate, Hadhramaut and the Sa'kal area in the east were the best places in Arabia to produce frankincense. Most was collected at Shabwah and taxed before being loaded onto caravans that carried it to the Mediterranean and Mesopotamia.

Hadhramaut was the entry point for Indian goods brought by sea and then shipped by land to Nagran. This trade may have suffered from competition by Red Sea shipping, as traders began to sail through the Bab El-Mandeb Strait into the Indian Ocean during the first century AD. Sabaean inscriptions suggest that the Hadramites were allies of the Sabaean Empire.

This oil painting by Italian artist Alberto Pasini depicts a caravan traveling in Arabia near the Red Sea. The actual painting may be found in the Galleria d'Arte Moderna in Florence, Italy.

4 POWER STRUGGLES

For centuries, the Minaeans, Sabaeans, Qatabanians, and Hadramites struggled to control ancient Arabia, but in the second century BC, powers shifted. The Minaean Empire, as well as parts of western Qataban, were conquered only by the Sabaeans.

The Romans

By the first century AD, the Romans began expanding their power and influence into the Red Sea. They learned how to exploit the monsoon winds to improve travel between the Red Sea and southern Asia, long a secret of Arab traders. In a short time, Arab prestige dwindled, since they could not compete in a trade war against the more powerful Romans. The resulting drop in income made it impossible for the Arabs to maintain their extensive cities.

Trade exploded in the Roman Empire, as shown on this map of ancient Roman trade routes surrounding the Arabian Peninsula, during the reign of Augustus, who led the empire from 27 BC until his death in AD 14. The Roman Empire imported corn for its rapidly growing populace, as well as luxury goods such as silk from China and ivory from Africa. The empire also made a practice of exporting goods, including olive oil and wine, throughout Asia.

Roman Trade Routes from 150 BC to AD 500

- Dura Europus
- Petra
- Muza
- Eudaemon Arabia
- Moscha

Tigris
Euphrates
Persian Gulf
RED SEA
Gulf of Aden

By AD 200, the Romans had conquered parts of northern Arabia. In AD 106, the Romans captured the capital at Petra, gaining control of the trade routes of the peninsula, to devastating effect. The change in trade served its purpose, however. In the long run, the Arabs traveling with the camel caravans were vital to the development of the Arabian Peninsula and Saudi Arabia.

The Himyarites

At around the same time, the Himyarites emerged in Arabia. While the Himyarites were an important tribe in the ancient Sabaean kingdom, they became the powerful rulers of much of southern Arabia from about 115 BC to AD 525.

The Himyarites were concentrated in the area known as Dhu Raydan on the present-day coast of the Republic of Yemen. They most likely aided in the overthrow of the Sabaeans by discovering a sea route from Egypt to India, which deprived the inland Sabaean kingdom of its importance as a trading center. The *Periplus Maris Erythraei*, a Greek seafaring manual written during the late first century AD, indicates the importance these shipping lanes had gained at the expense of the overland trade routes.

Upon conquering the Sabaeans, the Himyarites adopted the Sabaean language and culture. From their capital

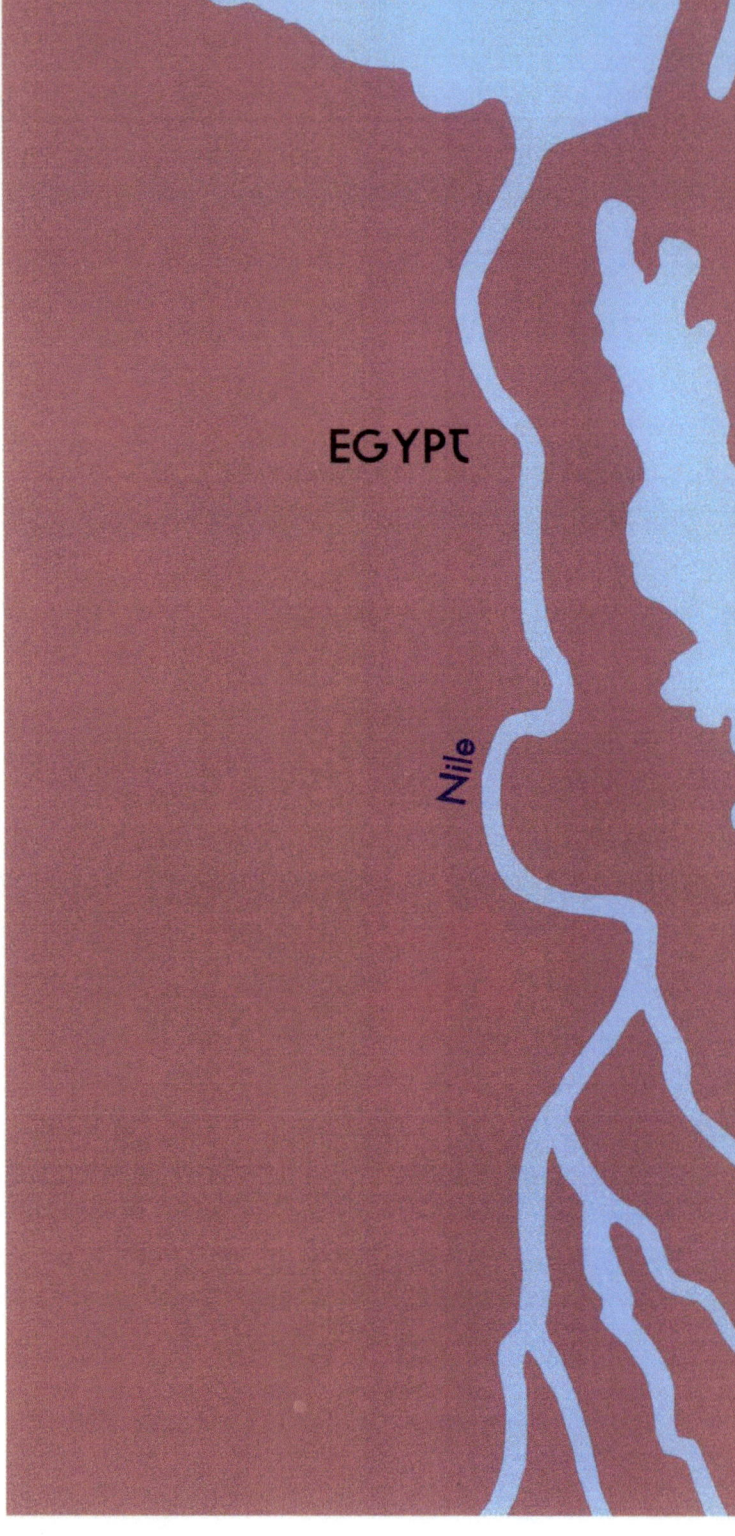

at Zafar, their power extended eastward as far as the Persian Gulf and northward into the Arabian Desert.

Late in the third century, Arabia consisted of only two empires: the Sabaean-Himyaric Empire in the west,

The Himyarites were a people that formed a concentrated settlement in an area known as Dhu Raydan, on the coast of the present-day Republic of Yemen. As a culture, the Himyarites inherited the Sabaean language and extended their might from their capital of Zafar (also spelled Sephar or Sapphar) eastward to the Persian Gulf and north to the Arabian Desert. By the fourth century AD, the Himyarites moved their capital north to San'a, before falling to Abyssinian control in AD 525.

and the kingdom of Hadhramaut extending from the former Qatabanian territory to Dhofar.

By the end of the third century, King Sammer Yuharis of Himyar set his sights on conquering Hadhramaut and southern Arabia. In a text from AD 295, Sammar Yuharis is referred to as the King of Saba. This indicates that, over time, he was successful against Hadhramaut and was able to unite southern Arabia into one empire. By the fourth century, the Himyar capital was moved northward to San'a.

One of the strongest rulers in Arabian history was Abukarib Asad, who came into power during the fifth century. Under his leadership, the Sabaean-Himyaric Empire expanded. He led military campaigns in central Arabia and as far as Yathrib. His official title was "King of Saba and Du-Raidan and Hadhramaut and Yamanat and their Arabs in the Highlands and on the Coast." This shows that the Arabian bedouins of the north, as well as the rural population of Yemen, had been incorporated into his empire.

The last Himyarite king was Yusuf As'ar Yath'ar (also known as Du Nuwas), who reigned in the sixth century. He launched military operations against the Abyssinian Christians in southern Arabia, killing many and destroying their fortresses. By AD 518, Nagran fell. Many Christians were put to death, evoking great sympathy throughout the Christian regions of Asia. This prompted the Abyssinians to prepare a military intervention in AD 523, led by Abyssinian king Ella Asbeha. Yusuf was killed, his army routed, and the area conquered. By AD 525, the Abyssinian invaders had crushed the Himyarites, marking the decline of the Sabaean-Himyaric Empire.

Conflicting clans and social tensions had made the region vulnerable to invasion. Incoming tribes from northern Arabia, poor agriculture, decreasing demand for frankincense from southern Arabia, and dwindling trade on the inland caravan routes all contributed to the fall of these ancient civilizations.

Other Tribes

Many smaller tribes thrived throughout the regions of the Arabian Peninsula. The tribal kingdoms of the Al-Hirah, the Ghassanids, the Kindah, and the Quraysh each had an impact on the evolution of power in Arabia.

Al-Hirah was a nomadic tribal kingdom whose kings were called the Lakhmids. The founder of the dynasty was Amr, whose son Imru' al-Qays died in AD 328. Imru' al-Qays

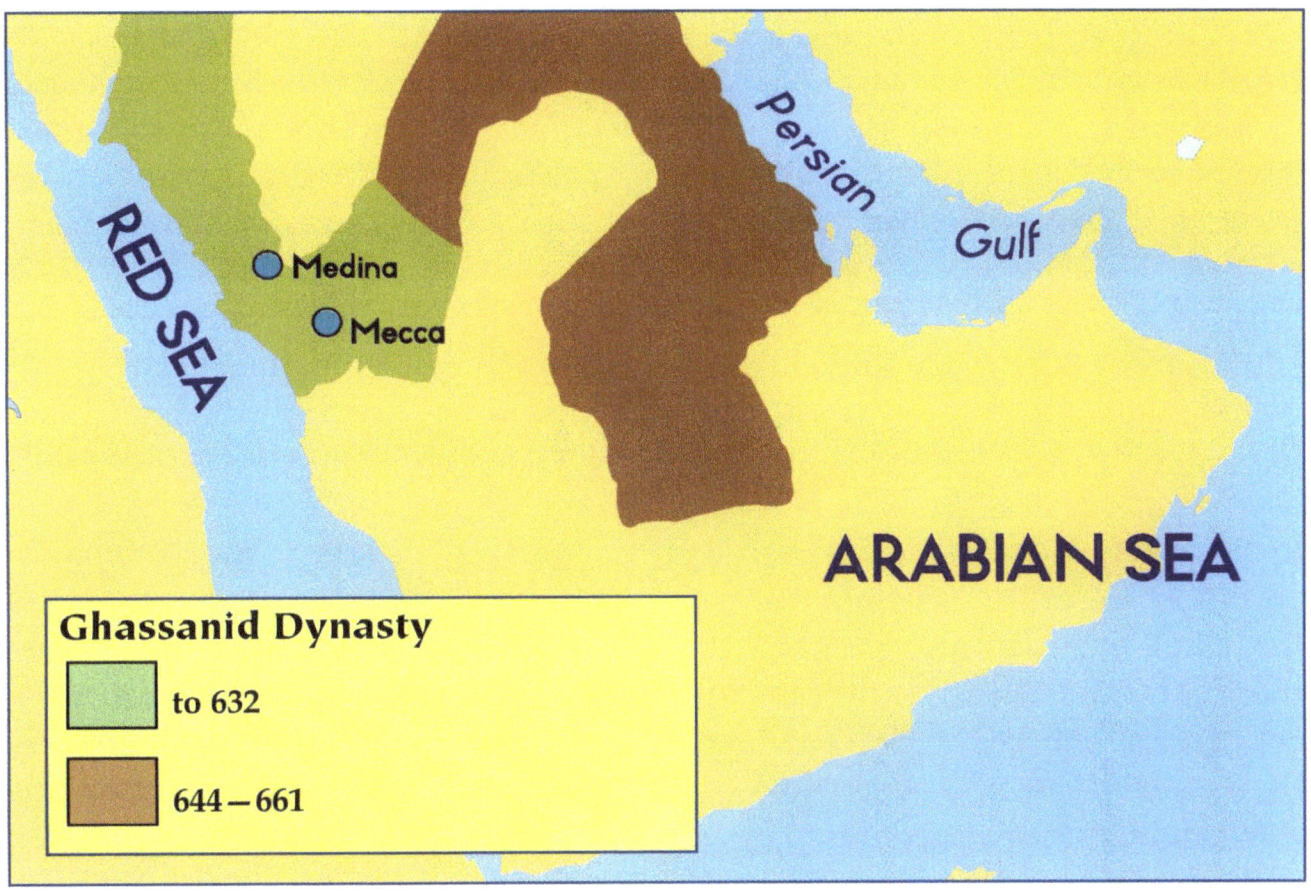

The Ghassanid dynasty was actually a collection of tribes and tribal leaders who together acted as a Roman vassal state (or subordinate servants) of the eastern portion of the Roman Empire. Today, the region that was once the Ghassanid dynasty, which was overthrown by Muslims in the seventh century, is located in Syria, Jordan, and Israel.

claimed the title of "king of all the bedouin" and campaigned successfully over the north and center of the Arabian Peninsula. He assumed leadership over the tribes of northeastern Arabia and tried to restrain their attacks. The Lakhmids remained influential throughout the sixth century, but in 602 the last Lakhmid king, Nu'man ibn al-Mundhir, was murdered by Sassanians, who were the rulers of Persia (Iran), and the Al-Hirah kingdom fell apart.

Ghassanid dynasty leaders are often called kings, though they were, in fact, Byzantine phylarchs, or native rulers of frontier states. They were based in the Byzantine Empire, east of the Sea of Galilee at Jabiyah in the Jawlan area, but they controlled areas of northwestern Arabia. They reigned as far south as Yathrib and often fought with the Lakhmids in the northeast. The Ghassanids were Christians who played a role in the religious conflicts of the Byzantine

Church before its destruction in 614 by the Persians.

Kindah was a tribal kingdom with influence in southern-central Arabia, from the Yemen border nearly as north as Mecca. The discovery of the tomb of a king of Kindah at Qaryat Dhat Kahil, on the trade route linking Najran with the eastern coast, suggests that this site was the kingdom's royal headquarters. Because Sabaean texts refer to Kindah in both friendly and hostile terms, scholars believe the Kindah traded and fought with them. This continued until the sixth century, when tribal wars caused the Kindah to collapse. Afterward, the powerful Quraysh emerged.

Quraysh was the ruling tribe of Mecca at the time of Muhammad's birth in AD 570. The tribe had ten main clans, including Hashim, the clan of Muhammad; Zuhra, that of his mother; Taim and 'Adi, the clans of the first and second caliphs, Abu Bakr and Umar, respectively; and Umayya, the clan of the third caliph, Uthman, who established the Umayyad dynasty.

Mecca had at one time been in the hands of the Jurhum, a people living on Arabia's western coast. Around 400, Mecca came under control of the Quraysh, whose clans improved the holy city. They took over control of the western trade routes, a role that had long before been played by the Minaeans and Nabataeans. They used their trading relationships with their bedouin cousins to develop Mecca into an influential city.

During the sixth century, the Quraysh reached agreements with other tribes, opening trade routes throughout the region. Under the Quraysh, caravans moved freely from Yemen to Mecca and north to Byzantium or east to Iraq.

In the opening years of the seventh century, the collapse of the Himyarites, Lakhmids, and Ghassanids left Arabia with little leadership. The Quraysh remained the only influence. Historians believe that these civilizations contributed to the eventual unification of the Islamic Empire.

5 THE RISE OF ISLAM

Saudi Arabians, as well as many other Arabs, trace their heritage to the birth of the prophet Muhammad in AD 570. The time before Islam is often referred to as "the time of ignorance," reflecting the fact that God had not yet sent the Arabs a prophet.

The Prophet Muhammad

Muhammad was born into the Quraysh, the leading tribe in the city of Mecca at a time when it was a young trading center. By that time, the Quraysh were active traders, having established alliances throughout the peninsula. Members of the Quraysh tribe were also wealthy, having received continual payments for offering protection to traveling caravans.

At the time, Arab tribes consisted of various clans. Muhammad came from a respectable clan, the sons of Hashim, but from a weak family. Muhammad's father, Abd Allah, had died before his son was born, and Muhammad was raised by both his grandfather and his uncle, who was one of the leaders of the Hashimite clan. This authority gave Muhammad some protection when he later began to preach.

Muhammad worked for his uncle in the caravan business, which allowed him to travel beyond Arabia and meet people in foreign Christian and Jewish communities. Despite this contact, Muhammad never

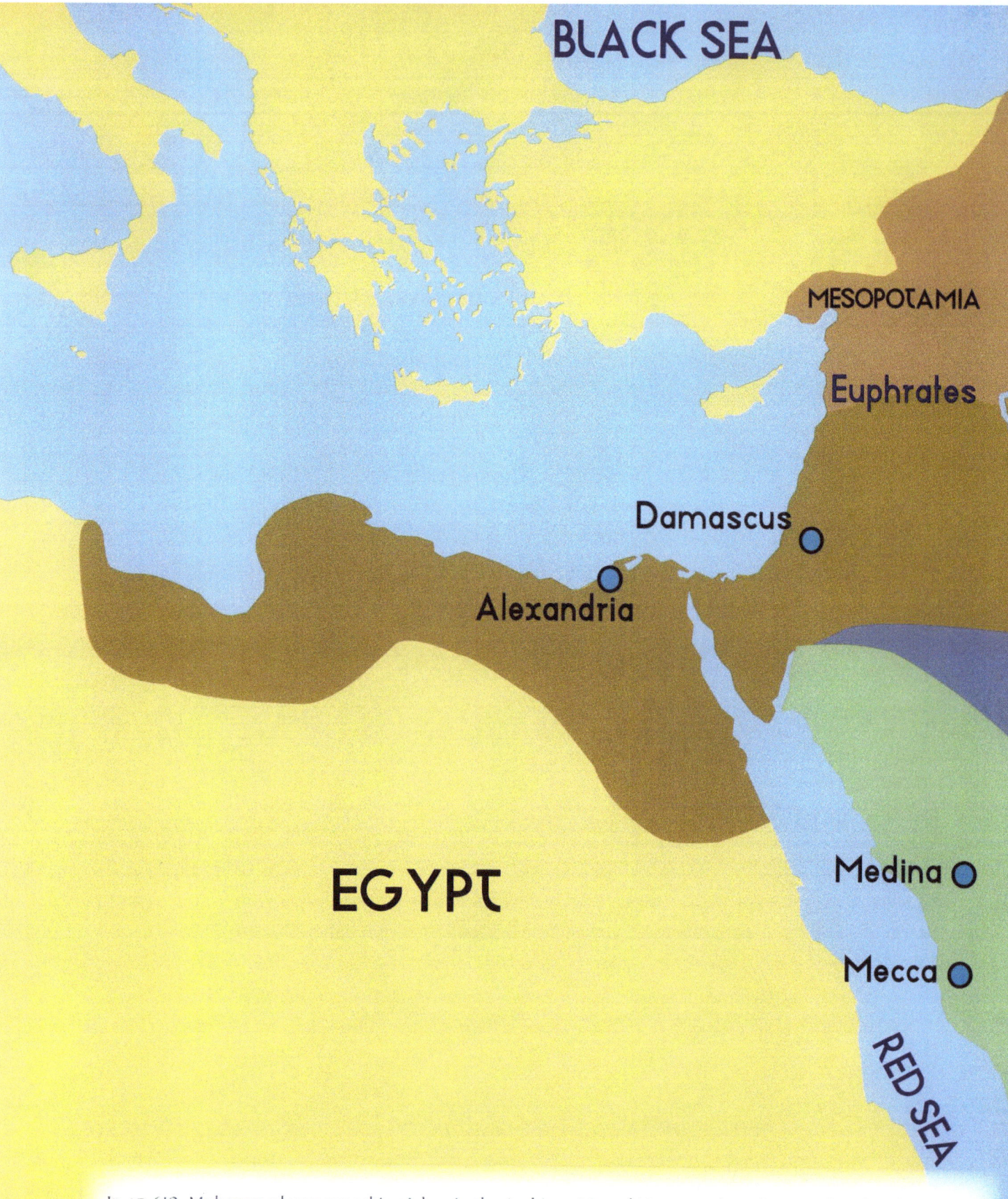

In AD 610, Muhammad was preaching Islam in the Arabian cities of Mecca and Medina. Within the short span of approximately thirty years, the religion had spread across the Red Sea to Egypt and later throughout most of Asia in every direction. Islam's message reached Syria in AD 635, Iraq in AD 637, Palestine in AD 640, Egypt in AD 642, and the entire Persian Empire in AD 650. Today Islam remains one of the world's great religions and is quickly becoming the world's most widely practiced, overtaking both Judaism and Christianity.

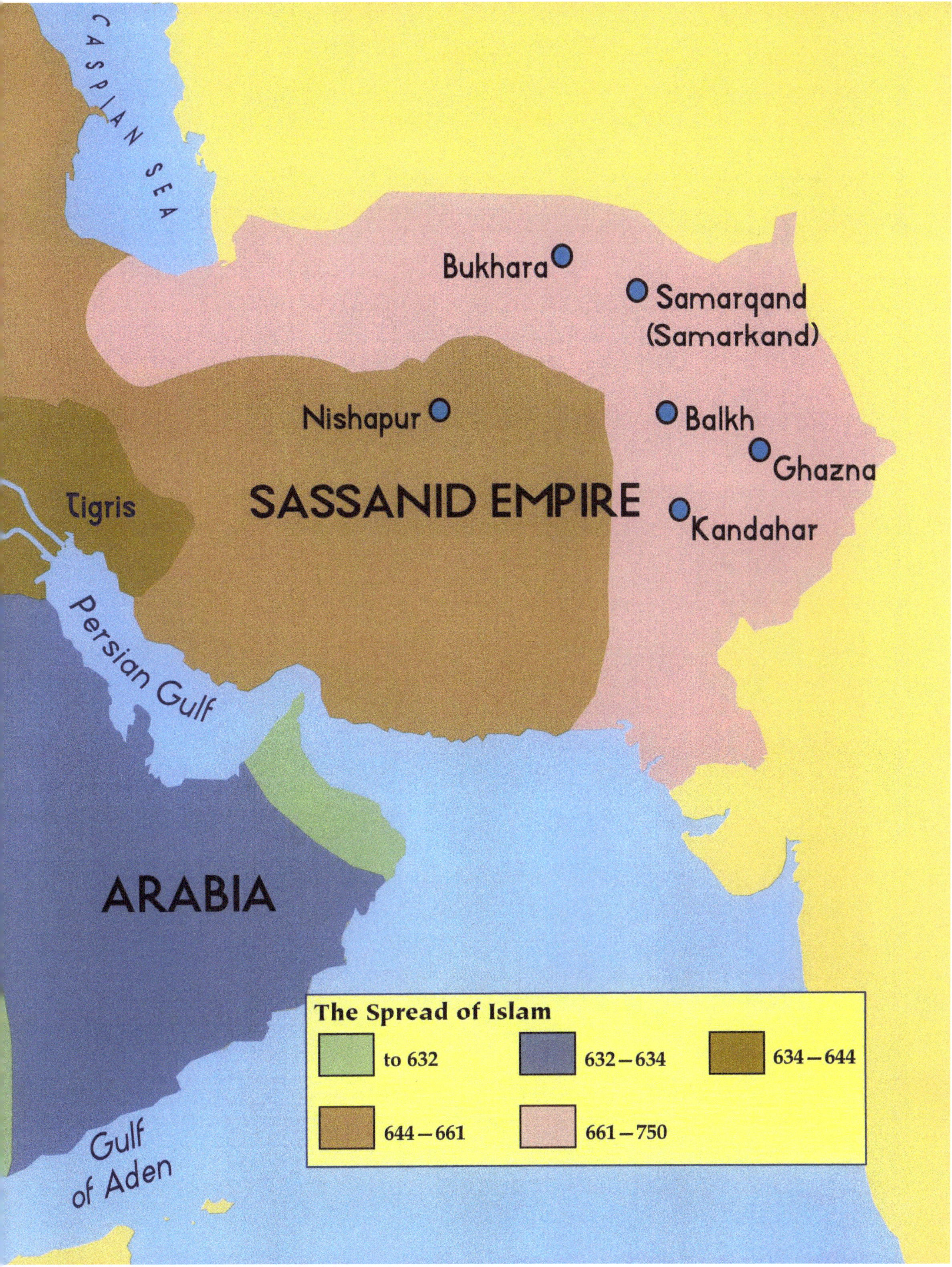

The Spread of Islam

- to 632
- 632–634
- 634–644
- 644–661
- 661–750

SASSANID EMPIRE

Bukhara, Samarqand (Samarkand), Nishapur, Balkh, Ghazna, Kandahar

ARABIA

Caspian Sea, Tigris, Persian Gulf, Gulf of Aden

learned to read or write. As a child he was sent to the desert for five years to learn the bedouin ways that were being forgotten in Mecca.

A New Faith

Muhammad married a rich widow named Khadija when he was twenty-five years old. Although he managed her business affairs, he would often isolate himself in the mountains. On one of these occasions, Muslim belief says that the angel Gabriel appeared to Muhammad and told him to recite aloud. When Muhammad asked what he should say, the angel recited for him verses that would later constitute part of the Koran (also spelled Qur'an), which literally means "the recitation." Muslims believe that Muhammad continued to receive revelations from God throughout his life, sometimes through the angel Gabriel and at other times directly from God.

The sixteenth-century Indian miniature painting seen here depicts the Ka'aba, or the most sacred house of God, in Mecca, which predates Islam and may have been built by Adam and rebuilt by Abraham. The Ka'aba is a stone cube structure that is covered in black cloth, as seen here, and confined in a restricted space called a haram, which only Muslims can enter.

For a while, Muhammad told only his wife about his experiences, but in 613 he acknowledged them openly and began to promote a new social and spiritual order based upon his revelations. Muhammad's message was disturbing to many of the Quraysh for several reasons. The most important of those was Muhammad's claim that there was only one God. Prior to the popularity of Islamic monotheism, the city of Mecca was a religious destination of Arab tribal members who worshiped many gods or idols. These polytheists traveled there to see the Ka'aba, a stone structure later known to Muslims as the House of Allah and God's first mosque on Earth. By condemning the worship of idols, Muhammad threatened pilgrimage traffic to Mecca that made the Quraysh wealthy.

By 618, Muhammad had gained enough followers to concern Mecca's leaders. Still, the Quraysh hesitated to harm him because of his connections to his powerful uncle. Instead, the Quraysh attacked his followers, who did not have family relationships of authority. To protect his supporters, Muhammad sent some of his followers to Ethiopia, where they were taken in by a Christian king As-Hama, who saw a relationship between Muhammad's ideas and those of his own.

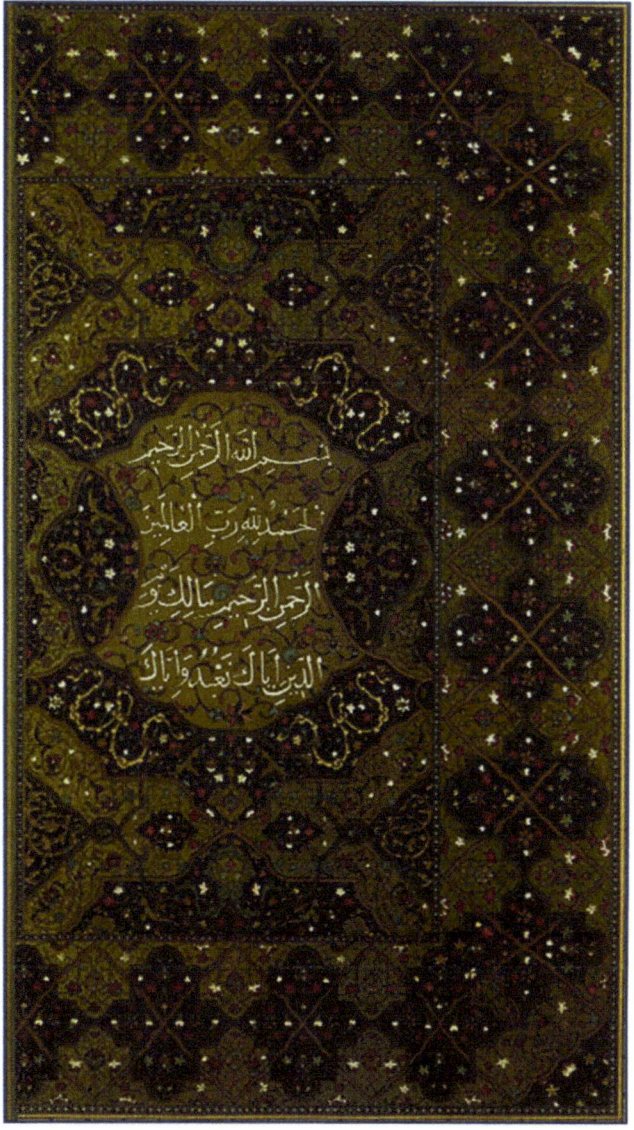

The sixteenth-century Arabic illumination shown here illustrates the first surah, known also as sura, of the Koran and is housed in a national library in Berlin, Germany.

Following his uncle's death in 619, and faced with growing hostility from the Quraysh, Muhammad decided to pursue his mission outside of Mecca, an event that was later linked to duty and sacrifice. He secretly slipped out of the city in AD 622 and traveled about 199 miles (320

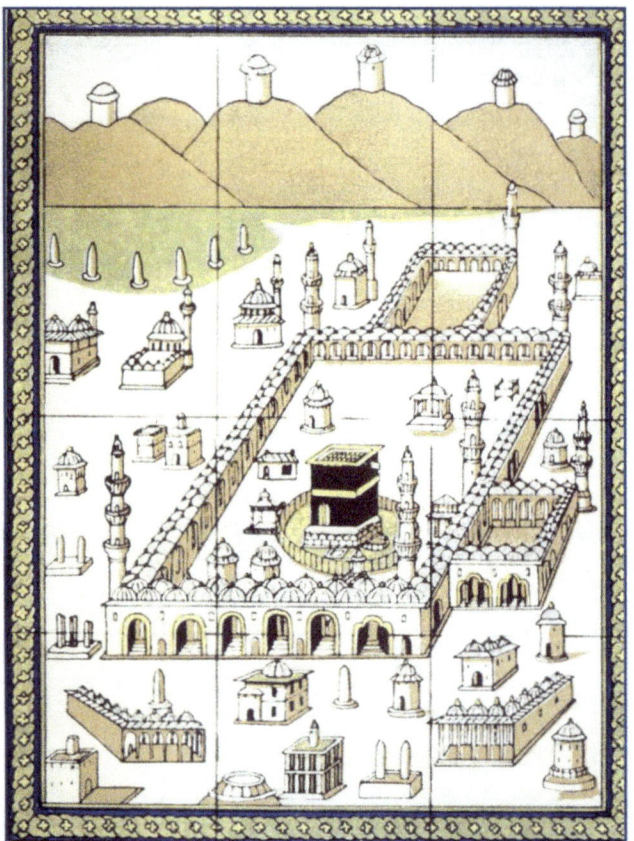

This illuminated medieval manuscript depicts the mosque surrounding the Ka'aba in Mecca, which continues to play a central role in the ritual life of all Muslims. Built as the first shrine for the worship of God, the Ka'aba is the focus of the Muslim pilgrimage to the city of Mecca.

kilometers) north to the town of Yathrib, present-day Medina. His emigration, called the *hijra*, marks the beginning of the Islamic calendar.

Yathrib is celebrated as the place from which Muhammad conquered all of Arabia after fleeing Mecca. The people of Yathrib welcomed Muhammad and adopted Islam, forming the first Islamic government in the world. The Quraysh lost two major battles against Muhammad and his followers, leading to a peace treaty. When the Quraysh broke the treaty, Muhammad gave them an ultimatum to submit to Islam or fight a holy war called a jihad.

Muhammad successfully led his growing army into Mecca in 630 and eventually attracted the loyalty of the entire Arabian Peninsula. If Muhammad's followers died after waging the jihad, they were promised a place in paradise. If they lived, they were guaranteed the wealth gained from having raided caravans and disrupting trade.

Abu Bakr

When Muhammad died in AD 632, Abu Bakr assumed his political functions as caliph, or successor, but it was probably under Umar ibn al-Khattab, the second caliph, that the term came into use as a title of the civil and religious head of the Muslim state. Caliphs ruled the Islamic world until AD 1258, when the last was killed by invading Mongol armies.

Abu Bakr, the first outside supporter of Muhammad, maintained the loyalty of the Arab tribes by force. He made it impossible for people to retain their traditional religious practices. Arabs who had previously converted to Judaism or Christianity were allowed to keep their religion, but those who tried to revert to old practices after Muhammad's death were forced to become Muslims. This is one of the central reasons that Islam became the religion of most Arabs.

The Caliphs

For the first thirty years after Muhammad's death, caliphs ruled the growing Islamic Empire from Yathrib, which had been renamed Madinat an-Nabi ("the city of the Prophet") or Al Madinah al Munawwarah ("the illuminated city"). This is usually shortened simply to Medina, which means "the city."

The caliphs channeled their energies against Roman and Persian territories and eventually conquered a vast empire. Arab-led armies pushed quickly through both of these empires and established Arab control from present-day Spain to Iran.

After the third caliph, Uthman, was assassinated in 656, the Muslim world was split, and the fourth caliph, Ali, was murdered in 660. After Ali, the Umayyads established a hereditary line of caliphs in Damascus. The 'Abbasids, a people who ruled from Baghdad (in modern-day Iraq), then overthrew the Umayyads in 750. By late in the seventh century, the political importance of Arabia in the Islamic world had declined.

Now housed in the Victoria and Albert Museum in London, England, this gouache painting depicts the third rightly guarded caliph, Uthman, seated with his Koran and rosary. It dates from the late eighteenth century, from the Deccan School of Indian painting.

The rise of Islam had huge influences on Arabia and the Arabian Peninsula as a whole. It led the people toward a new way of life. This fervor made it possible for Arab armies to increasingly conquer territory during the seventh century.

6 ARABIA AFTER MUHAMMAD

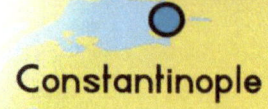

Until about 900, the center of Islamic power remained in the Fertile Crescent, the semicircle of land extending from the southeastern Mediterranean coast around the Syrian Desert north of the Arabian Peninsula to the Persian Gulf. After the ninth century, however, political centers moved into present-day Egypt, India, Turkey, and the central Asian republics. Islamic civilization was no longer centered in Mecca and Medina.

However, Mecca remained the spiritual center of Islam because it was the destination for the hajj that all Muslims must try to make once in their lives. The city, however, lacked political importance even in the early Islamic period. Medina, once the base for Muhammad's efforts to bring together the tribes of the Arabian Peninsula, had become its intellectual and literary center.

Muslim conquests in Arabia were chaotic after the death of the prophet Muhammad in AD 632. Abu Bakr became the first caliph, but tribes throughout Arabia discontinued sending tribute payments (taxes) to Medina in a conflict known as the Wars of Apostasy. Despite the grievances, the expansion of the Muslim Empire continued. Beginning in AD 636, Muslim armies defeated the Persians, reached Damascus in AD 637, and extended forces in all directions into present-day Iraq, Syria, and Egypt.

From the time of Muhammad's death there had been a controversy over succession. A minority called the Shiite Muslims believed that Ali should have led the Muslim community immediately after Muhammad. They were frustrated several times, however, when the larger Muslim community selected first Abu Bakr, then Umar, and then Uthman, as caliph. When Ali finally became caliph in AD 656, the Shiites refused to accept claims to the caliphate from other Muslim leaders, such as Muawiyah from Syria.

Ali's election as caliph was challenged, leading to a war between Muawiyah's and Ali's supporters. Muawiyah and Ali eventually agreed to an arbitrator, and the fighting stopped. Part of Ali's army, however, objected to the compromise, claiming Muawiyah's family was insincere. Strong in their protest against compromise, they left Ali's camp and founded the Kharijite movement. The term *khariji* literally means "the ones who leave."

The Kharijite Movement

The Kharijite movement's most prominent quality was opposition to the caliph's representatives and particularly to Muawiyah, who became caliph after Ali. Although the Kharijites were a minority regarded as bandits and assassins, they developed certain notions of justice and religious devotion. According to the Kharijites, whoever didn't follow Muhammad's directives should be opposed, shunned, or killed.

The Kharijites' religious fanaticism is but one example of the fervor with which the tribal Arabs had accepted Islam, a spirit that enabled Arab armies to lead and conquer so much territory. This same zeal later helped the Al Sa'ud succeed at the end of the eighteenth century and again at the beginning of the twentieth century.

The dispute between Muawiyah and Ali was never fully resolved. Muawiyah returned to Syria while Ali went to Iraq, where he was assassinated in AD 660. Muawiyah assumed the caliphate, while Ali's supporters transferred their loyalty to Ali's two sons, Hasan and Husayn. Although Hasan declined to challenge Muawiyah, Husayn was less timid. When Muawiyah's son, Yazid, succeeded his father, Husayn refused to recognize his authority. He set out for Iraq to raise support but was intercepted by a force loyal to Yazid. When Husayn refused to surrender, his entire party was killed at Karbala in southeastern Iraq.

The killing of Husayn led to the emergence of the Shiite as a distinct sect of Islam. Eventually, the Shiite sect split into several separate

Arabia After Muhammad

The manuscript pictured on this page was taken from *al-Hariri's Maqamat* (Assemblies, or Entertaining Dialogues) and was painted by al-Wasiti in Baghdad in AD 1237. It illustrates the farewells of Abou Zayd and Al Harith before their return to Mecca and is presently housed in the National Library of France in Paris.

divisions based on disputes over who of Ali's descendants should be the true spiritual leader. The majority, called Sunni Muslims, came to recognize a line of twelve leaders, or imams, beginning with Ali and ending with Muhammad al Muntazar.

The smaller Shiite minority in Saudi Arabia traces its origin to the days of Ali. A second Shiite group, the Ismailis, follow a line of imams that originally challenged the seventh imam and supported a younger brother, Ismail. The Ismaili line of leaders has been continuous to the present day. The current imam, Sadr ad Din Agha Khan, is a direct descendant of Ali.

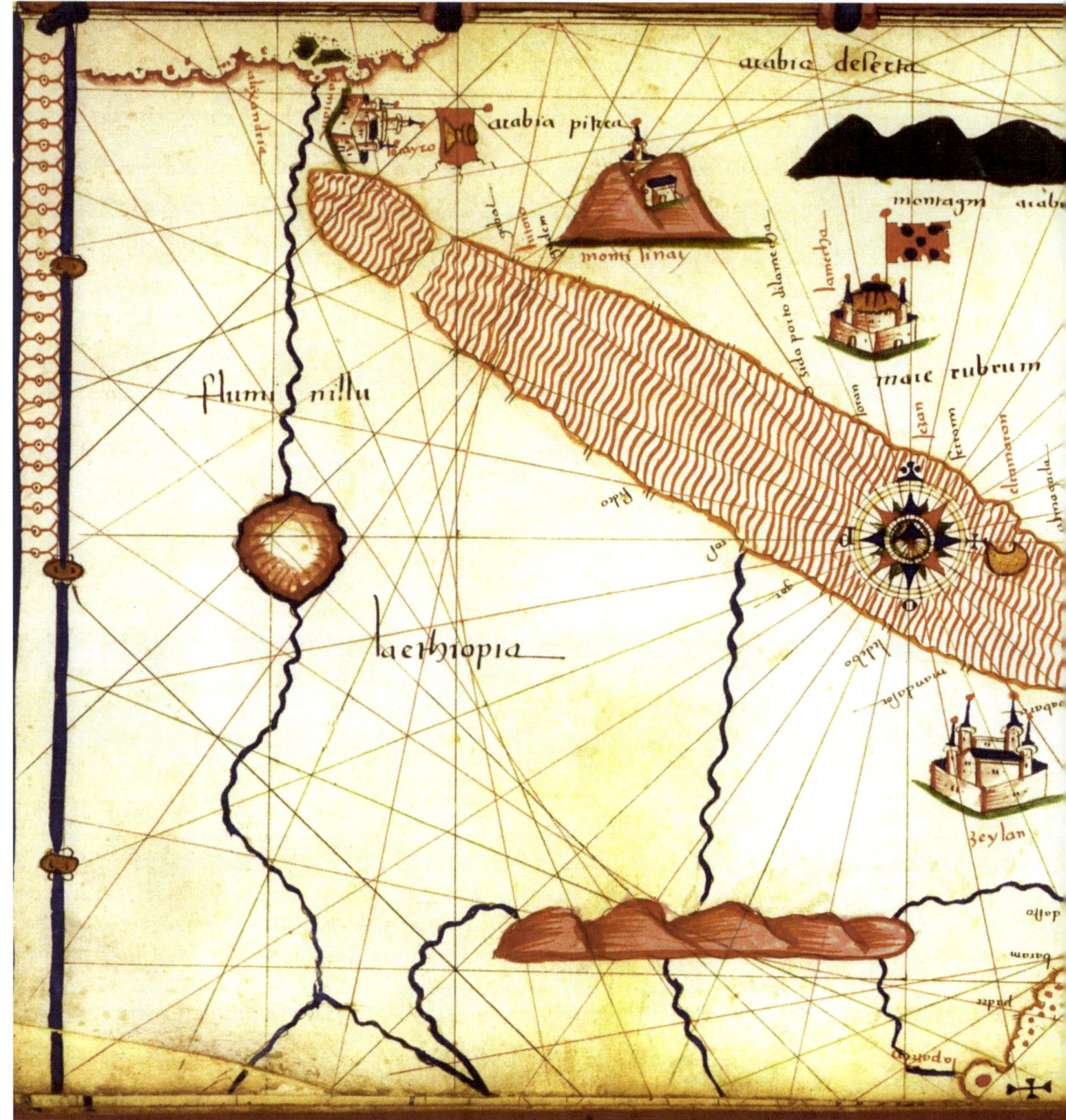

This colorful fifteenth-century map of Egypt and the Red Sea was drawn by Jacopo Russo. It is currently housed at a library in Modena, Italy.

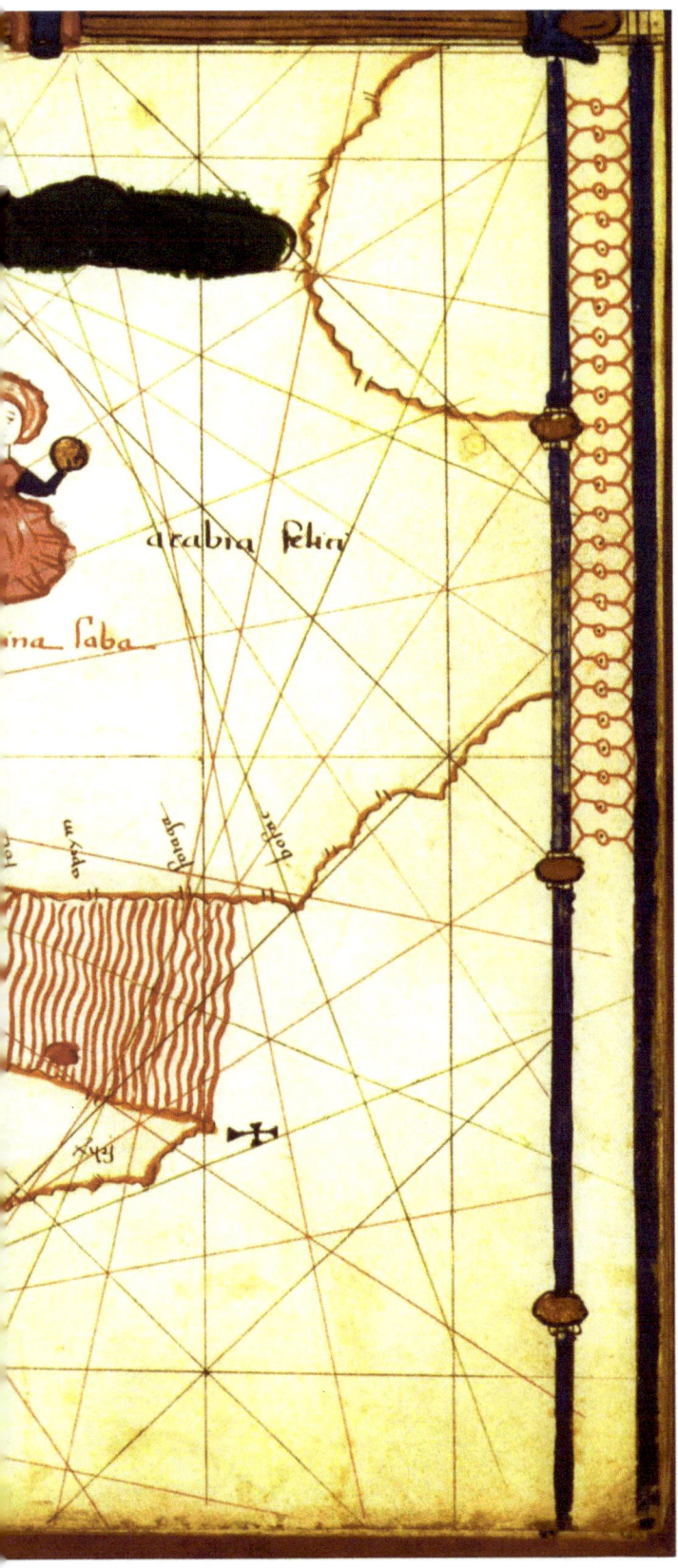

Under normal circumstances, Muslims visited Mecca each year for the hajj. They expected the caliph to keep the pilgrimage routes safe and to maintain control over Mecca, Medina, and the Red Sea ports providing access to them. When the caliph was strong, he controlled the Hijaz, the western coastal region of Arabia on the Red Sea, but after the ninth century, the caliph's power weakened and the Hijaz became a target.

External control of the Hijaz gave the region contact with other parts of the Muslim world mainly because of the merchant sailors who imported and exported goods from the port cities there. In order to reach the Hijaz, one traveled through the Najd, the barren region to the east. As the caliphs in Baghdad became less powerful, the road between Baghdad and Mecca that led across the Najd declined in importance. After the thirteenth century, pilgrimage traffic was more likely to move up the Red Sea toward Egypt and bypass the Najd, which to this day remains isolated.

This led to two factions in Arabian Islam. To the west was the Hijaz, which derived a cosmopolitan quality from its foreign travelers. During the eighteenth century, Wahhabism, or ideas associated with a Muslim sect founded by Muhammad ibn 'Abd al-Wahhab (1703–1792) that focused on strict observance of the Koran, would originate in the Najd. Later, Wahhabism would be vital to the rise of the Al Sa'ud, the ruling dynasty of Saudi Arabia.

41

7 THE WAHHABIS AND THE HOUSE OF SA'UD

The history of modern Saudi Arabia can be broken into three periods. The first begins in the mid-eighteenth century with the alliance between Muhammad ibn Sa'ud and Muhammad ibn 'Abd al-Wahhab and ends with the capture of Abd Allah. The second period extends from this point to the rise of Abd al-Aziz ibn Sa'ud II, the founder of the modern state; the third consists of the establishment and present history of the Kingdom of Saudi Arabia.

Wahhab and Al-Sa'ud Unite

The house of Sa'ud, or Al-Sa'ud, began in Ad Diriyah, in the center of the Najd close to Riyadh. The ancestors of Muhammad ibn Sa'ud settled there to raise dates, one of the few fruits that the dry region could support.

This map, which shows Ottoman territories in Arabia and Egypt from the nineteenth to twentieth centuries, illustrates how Turkish power declined during this period. Although the Turks had gained control of eastern Arabia (including the present-day Republic of Yemen) during the sixteenth century and adopted the religion of Islam, by 1804, the Ottomans were in control only of the Hijaz region, the section of Saudi Arabia that contains the holy cities of Mecca and Medina. This was largely because their empire had become overextended and their power to control such a wide region had weakened. By 1768, Ottoman forces were also engaged in a war with the Russians, a conflict that would last until 1774.

Over time, the area developed into a small town led by the Sa'ud clan.

Like it was explained in the previous chapter, the rise of Al-Sa'ud is closely linked with the Wahhabi movement. Muhammad ibn 'Abd al-Wahhab was a Muslim scholar whose ideas about Islam formed the basis of Wahhabism. He grew up in Uyaynah, an oasis in the southern Najd, where he studied strict Hanbali Islamic law. While he was young, he left Uyaynah to study with other teachers, the usual way to pursue education in the Islamic world. He studied in Medina and then went to Iraq and Iran.

On his travels, 'Abd al-Wahhab met Shiite Muslims and encountered other Arabian tribes worshiping more liberal interpretations of Islam. This disturbed him greatly. In the late 1730s, he went to the Najdi town of Huraymila to write and preach against both Shiite and local Muslim practices. He focused on the principle that there is only one God and that God does not share his power with anyone, people or objects. From this principle, his students began to refer to themselves as *muwahhidun*, or reformed unitarians. People opposing their religious opinions referred to them as "Wahhabis," the followers of 'Abd al-Wahhab, which to them was an insult.

Lacking political support in Huraymila, 'Abd al-Wahhab returned to Uyaynah, where he attracted local attention. The leaders of nearby Al Hufuf were alarmed by the anti-Shiite tone of the Wahhabis. 'Abd al-Wahhab was thrown out of Uyaynah and headed to

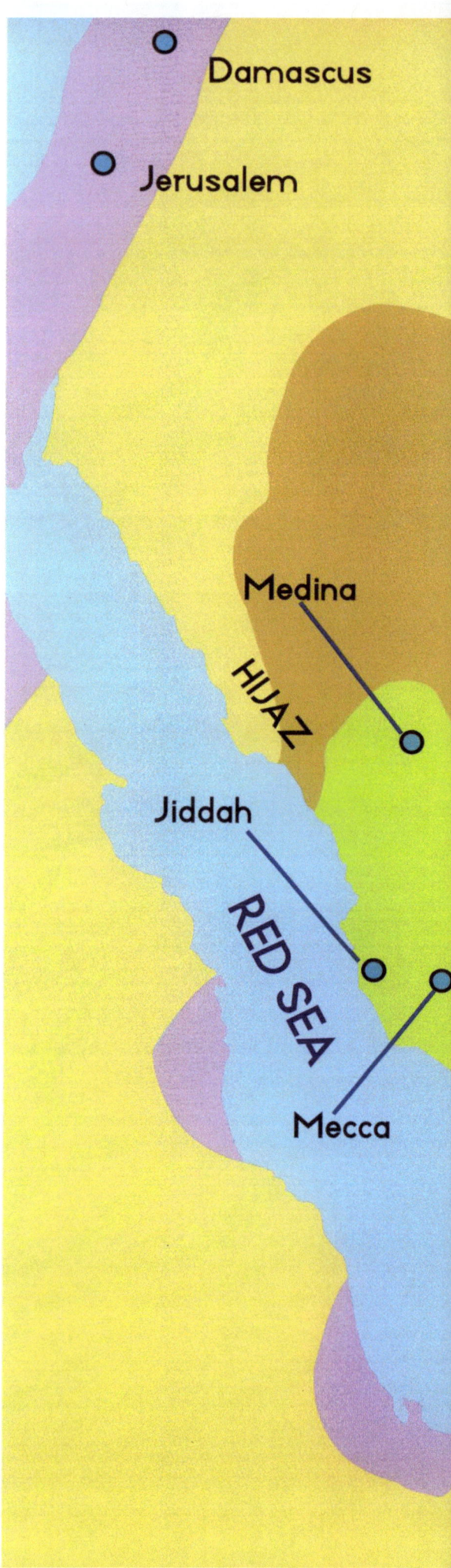

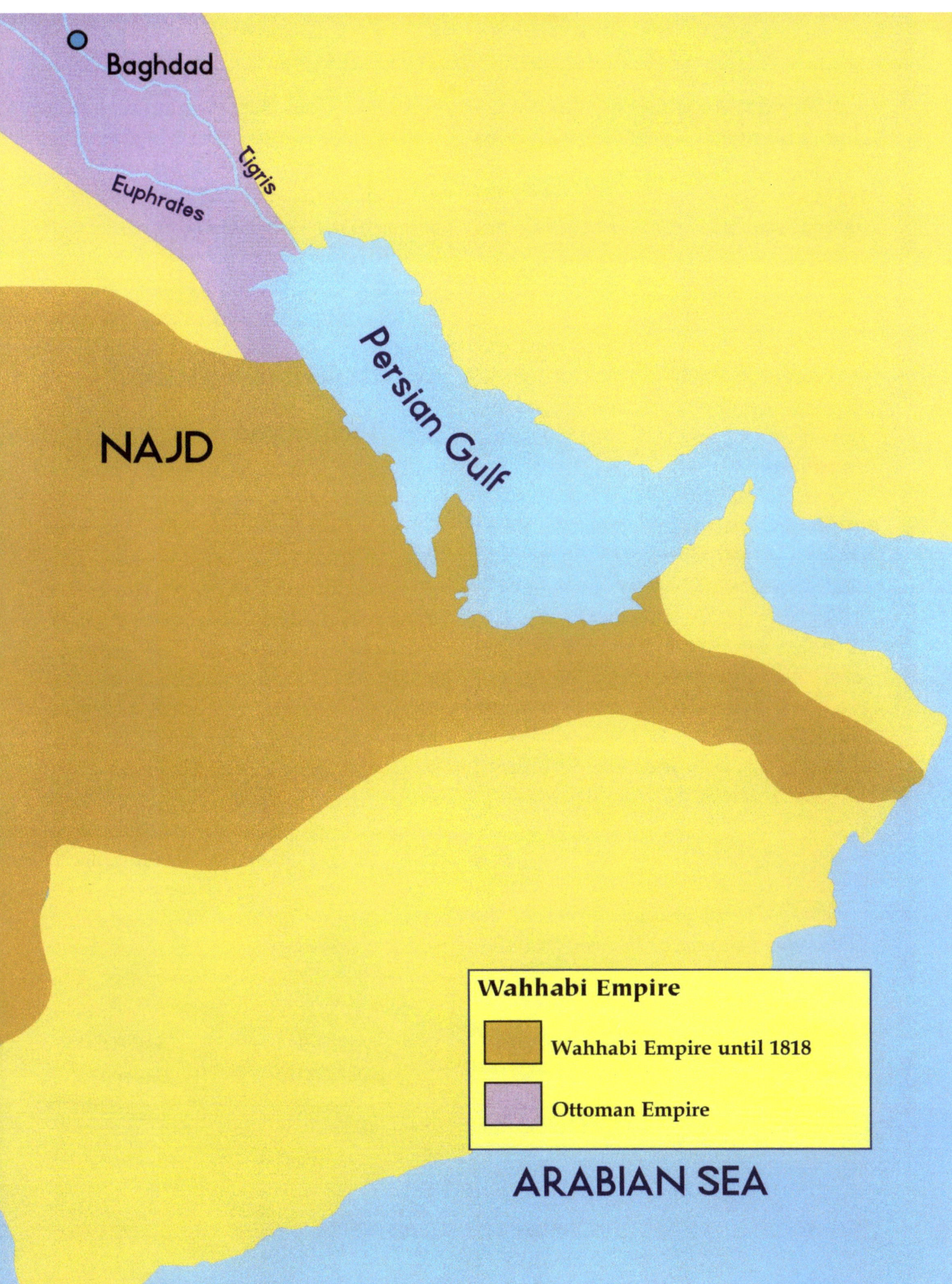

Ad Diriyah, some forty miles (sixty-four kilometers) away, which was the seat of Muhammad ibn Sa'ud. He had made contact with ibn Sa'ud earlier, and two of his brothers went with him when he destroyed shrines around Uyaynah.

When 'Abd al-Wahhab arrived in Ad Diriyah, ibn Sa'ud was ready to support him. In 1744, they promised to work together to establish a nation governed according to strict Islamic principles.

Ibn Sa'ud led armies into Najdi towns and villages to eliminate Shiite practices. By 1765, his forces had established Wahhabism, and with it ibn Sa'ud's political authority.

After ibn Sa'ud died in 1765, his son and successor, Abd al-Aziz I (reigned 1765–1803), continued to work with 'Abd al-Wahhab. Abd al-Aziz I continued the Wahhabi advance until his death at age eighty-nine.

In 1801, the Sa'ud-Wahhabi armies attacked Karbala, a Shiite shrine in Ottoman-controlled Iraq. In 1803, the Wahhabis moved to take control of Sunni towns in the Ottoman-controlled Hijaz. One year later, Sa'ud-Wahhabi forces captured Mecca and Medina in the Hijaz.

Capturing the Hijaz brought the Sa'ud Empire into conflict with the rest of the Islamic world. The Shiite practices that the Wahhabis hated were important to other Muslims, the majority of whom were alarmed that local shrines were destroyed and their access to the holy cities was restricted. In addition, taking the Hijaz was symbolically important. The Ottoman Turks, the most important political force in the Islamic world at the time, refused to concede the Hijaz.

The Ottomans

Although the Wahhabi attacks attracted the attention of the Ottoman government, the area was still under its leadership. The Ottoman Empire at its height in the sixteenth century, also ruled most of southeastern Europe. The empire, which stretched northwest to the gates of Vienna, included present-day Hungary, Serbia, Bosnia, Romania, Greece, the Ukraine, Iraq, Syria, Israel, and Egypt, North Africa as far west as Algeria, and most of the Arabian Peninsula. At the beginning of the nineteenth century, however, the Ottomans were not in a position to forcefully recover the Hijaz from the Wahhabis. The empire had been in decline for more than two centuries. Its forces were weak and overextended.

Instead, the Ottomans entrusted the recapture of the Hijaz to Muhammad Ali, the governor of

This map of the Ottoman Empire, showing its growth during the Golden Age (1481–1566), illustrates acquired Muslim lands beginning in the sixteenth century under Selim I (reigned 1512–1520), who, after his victory, took the title of caliph. Selim I, known as Selim the Grim, gained control of all Middle Eastern trade routes between Europe and Asia that were previously controlled by Muslims. The Ottoman conquest of Arabia would last until the early nineteenth century.

Egypt. Ali, with his son Tursun, recaptured the Hijaz after a seven-year battle. Abd al-Aziz's grandson, Abd Allah, faced the invading Egyptian army but was defeated and forced to retreat to the Najd.

Ali pursued him there, sending out another army under the command of his other son, Ibrahim. The Wahhabis retreated to the Sa'ud capital of Ad Diriyah, where they managed to hold out for two years against superior Egyptian forces and weaponry. In the end, however, the Wahhabis proved no match for the Egyptian army, and Ad Diriyah fell in 1818.

The Egyptians

In the Egyptians' attempt to control the peninsula, Muhammad Ali removed members of the Sa'ud family from the area. Following orders from the Ottoman sultan, he had Abdullah Ibn Saud, the Wahhabi leader of the time, beheaded and forced the family into exile.

The Egyptians destroyed the city of Ad Diriyah and captured Al Qatif, a port on the Persian Gulf that supplied eastern Arabia. They also maintained forces along the Red Sea coast.

In the Hijaz, Ali restored the authority of the sharifs, who had ruled the area since the tenth century. However, Turki ibn Abd Allah, a grandson of ibn Sa'ud, upset Egyptian efforts at control. Abd Allah had fought at Ad Diriyah but managed to escape the Egyptians when the town fell in 1818. He hid for a time and then recaptured Ad Diriyah in 1821. From the ruins of Ad Diriyah, Abd Allah proceeded to Riyadh, the city that eventually became the Sa'udi base. Forces under his control reclaimed the rest of the Najd in 1824 and expelled the Egyptians.

Abd Allah's relatively swift conquest of the Najd indicated the growth of support for and the authority of the Sa'ud-Wahhabi partnership. The successes of the Wahhabi forces promoted tribal loyalty to Al-Sa'ud.

Turki had tried to maintain friendly ties with the Ottoman governors of Iraq as well as the British, a country that became increasingly concerned about Ali's control in the region, especially control over trade routes between Europe and India. Turki and his successors ruled over too wide an area, controlling the region to the north and south of the Najd and exerted considerable influence along the western coast of the Persian Gulf. This was not a state, but a large sphere of influence that the Sa'udis held together with treaties and delegated authority.

The Al-Sa'ud dynasty recruited troops for various campaigns. The rulers described them as holy wars, which they conducted according to Islamic principles. Al-Sa'ud also demanded a tribute (tax) be paid by those under their control, as the laws of Islam commanded.

Strict Wahhabi religious beliefs had even spread through the central part of the Arabian Peninsula. As a result, Al-Sa'ud also influenced

---

British interests in Saudi Arabia steadily increased throughout the twentieth century after the construction of the Suez Canal in 1869. The canal, a successful engineering project that decreased travel time between Europe and India (a country then occupied by the British) and increased trading between the East and West, further encouraged British interests in the region. Gradually, British leaders gained control over the entire South Arabian coast by entering into various relationships with Saudi sheiks who preferred protection of their shores by British over Ottoman or Wahhabi forces. Eventually, those agreements resulted in at least twenty separate protectorate treaties.

decisions in areas not under its control, such as local battles and tribute payments. Al-Sa'ud's influence in the Hijaz, however, remained restricted. Not only were the Egyptians and Ottomans careful that the region not slip away again, but Wahhabi ideas had not yet found a receptive audience in western Arabia.

Al-Sa'ud Versus the Ottomans

The Al-Sa'ud dynasty had a genuine problem in the Ottomans. The challenge to the Turkish sultan had helped end the first Sa'ud kingdom in 1818, so later rulers tried to accommodate the Ottomans as best they could. Al-Sa'ud eventually became important to the Ottomans. Since the Sa'udis collected tributes from Oman, and forwarded much of this to the sharifs in Mecca, the Ottoman sultan eventually benefitted from these payments. In return, the Ottomans recognized Al-Sa'ud authority and left them alone.

However, the Turks sometimes tried to exert their influence by supporting renegade members of the Sa'udis. When Abd Allah's grandsons vied to take over the empire from their father, Abd Allah enlisted the aid of the Ottoman governor in Iraq, who used the opportunity to take control of eastern Arabia. The Turks were eventually driven out, but until the time of Abd al-Aziz II, they continued to exploit differences within the Sa'ud family.

Abd al-Aziz ibn Sa'ud, king of Saudi Arabia from 1880 to 1953, was photographed in 1922 during the Desert War.

The leadership changed hands seven times over the next five years as different members of the Sa'ud family wrested control in a civil war. When a drought from 1870 to 1874 devastated the region, the Wahhabi leadership also broke down.

While the Sa'udis were bickering, the family of Muhammad ibn Rashid, who controlled the area around the Shammar Mountains, grew stronger and expanded its influence in the northern Najd. Abd Allah was captured by Ibn Rashid at Hail, while a representative of the Rashidis was appointed governor of Riyadh in 1887. Abd Allah, however,

The British

One of the reasons the Ottomans were unsuccessful in controlling the Sa'ud was the growing British interest in Arabia. The British government in India considered the Persian Gulf to be its western flank and so became involved with the Arab tribes on the eastern coast. The British were also anxious about potentially hostile Ottoman influence in an area so close to India and the Suez Canal. As a result, the British worked with the Sa'ud. As Wahhabi leaders, the Sa'udis could exert some control over the tribes on the Gulf Coast, and they were simultaneously involved with the Ottomans. During this period, Sa'udi leaders began to play the Ottomans and British against each other. While the Sa'udis were successful in handling the two great powers in the Persian Gulf, they did not do so well in managing their own family affairs.

was allowed to return to Riyadh and was named governor of the city in 1889. Unfortunately, he died the same year, leaving his youngest brother, Abd ar-Rahman, the difficult task of ruling.

Abd ar-Rahman was soon fighting with the Rashidis, who defeated the Wahhabis in the Battle of Al-Mulaida in 1891. As a result, the Wahhabi state was destroyed. Abd ar-Rahman and Sa'ud, along with his young son Abd al-Aziz II, also known as ibn Sa'ud, had to take refuge with the sheik of Kuwait. But Abd al-Aziz II would later return to Arabia for vengeance.

8 MODERN SAUDI ARABIA

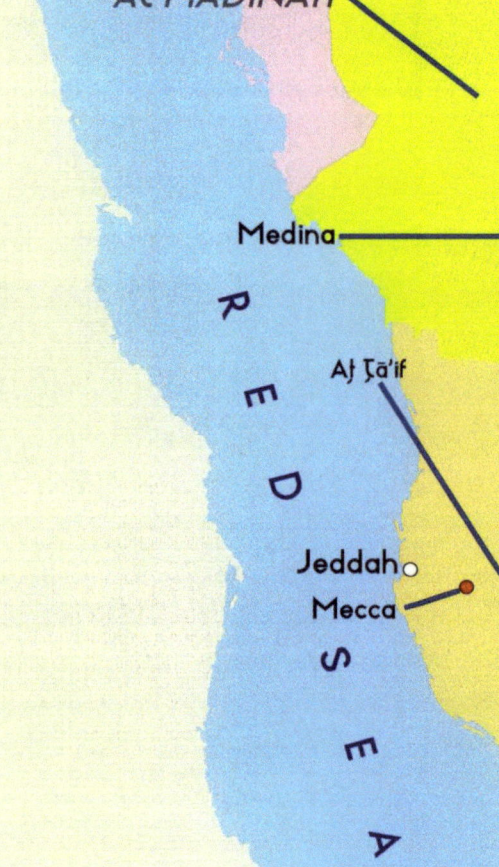

Abd al-Aziz II was the tribal and Muslim religious leader who formed the modern state of Arabia and started oil exploration. He established the Sa'udi state in three stages: He retook the Najd in 1905, defeated the Rashidi clan at Hail in 1921, and conquered the Hijaz in 1924.

In 1901, Abd al-Aziz II, then twenty-one, set out from Kuwait to regain his family's lands. He invaded Riyadh and defeated the Rashidis. From his seat in Riyadh, Abd al-Aziz II made peace with some tribes and fought with others. He eventually strengthened his position so that the Rashidi were unable to evict him. By 1905, the Ottoman governor in Iraq recognized Abd al-Aziz II as an Ottoman client in the Najd. The Sa'ud ruler accepted Turkish rule because it improved his political position.

In 1902, Abd al-Aziz ibn Sa'ud had captured Riyadh, a move that would set the pace for the unification of the Saudi Peninsula for the next thirty years. By the 1930s, the discovery of oil in the Kingdom of Saudi Arabia transformed the country into an independent nation of great wealth. Today, modern Saudi Arabia, as seen on this map, is a political ally of the United States, and relations with its leaders, King and Prime Minister Fahd bin Abd al-Aziz Al-Sa'ud and his brother, Crown Prince and First Deputy Prime Minister Abdullah bin Abd al-Aziz Al-Sa'ud, are stable.

Secretly, however, he asked the British to rid Arabia of Ottoman influence. Finally, in 1913, and without British assistance, Abd al-Aziz II's armies drove the Turks out of eastern Arabia.

The Ikhwan Movement

To revive support for Wahhabism, Abd al-Aziz II allied with tribes called the Ikhwan in 1912. He was a devout Muslim and his life was regulated by the Koran. A savvy leader, he knew that religious fanaticism could serve his ambition well. He encouraged his followers to massacre Arab rivals, helping him control many nomadic tribesmen.

Abd al-Aziz II organized the Ikhwan bedouin into an elite army corps. In order to break their traditional ways, he settled them around desert oases in colonies known as *hijrahs*. The hijrahs offered tribesmen shelter, mosques, schools, agricultural instruction, and firearms. Most important, religious teachers instructed them in the kind of Islam taught by 'Abd al-Wahhab. The Ikhwan became extreme fundamentalists. By 1918, they joined Abd al-Aziz's elite army.

In 1919, the Ikhwan began a campaign against the Hashimid kingdom on Arabia's northwestern coast. They defeated Husayn ibn 'Ali at Turabah in 1919. In 1924, they moved against Jordan, Iraq, and the Hijaz. Mecca fell to the Ikhwan, and Jeddah and Medina surrendered in 1925. But by 1926, the Ikhwan were out of control.

Abd al-Aziz had problems establishing the kingdom of Arabia, but ironically, the first and most serious of these was the Ikhwan, once his most ardent supporters. They began to criticize Abd al-Aziz for introducing modern implements such as telephones, automobiles, and the telegraph. The Ikhwan became militant in their Muslim beliefs and attacked those who disagreed with them.

The Ikhwan forced their religious beliefs on anyone who did not accept them. This led them to attack non-Wahhabi Muslims and occasionally Wahhabi Muslims within Arabia, forcing them to flee to Iraq. The attacks not only challenged Abd al-Aziz's authority, but they caused him problems with British leaders who would not tolerate the violation of new, post–World War I borders.

Ibn Sa'ud spoke directly to the Muslim people and convinced many of them to fight. When the Wahhabi forces continued to ignore Abd al-Aziz, he waged a bloody battle and defeated them in 1929. Many sided with him, setting the foundation of the modern state. Later, they became the Saudi Arabian National Guard.

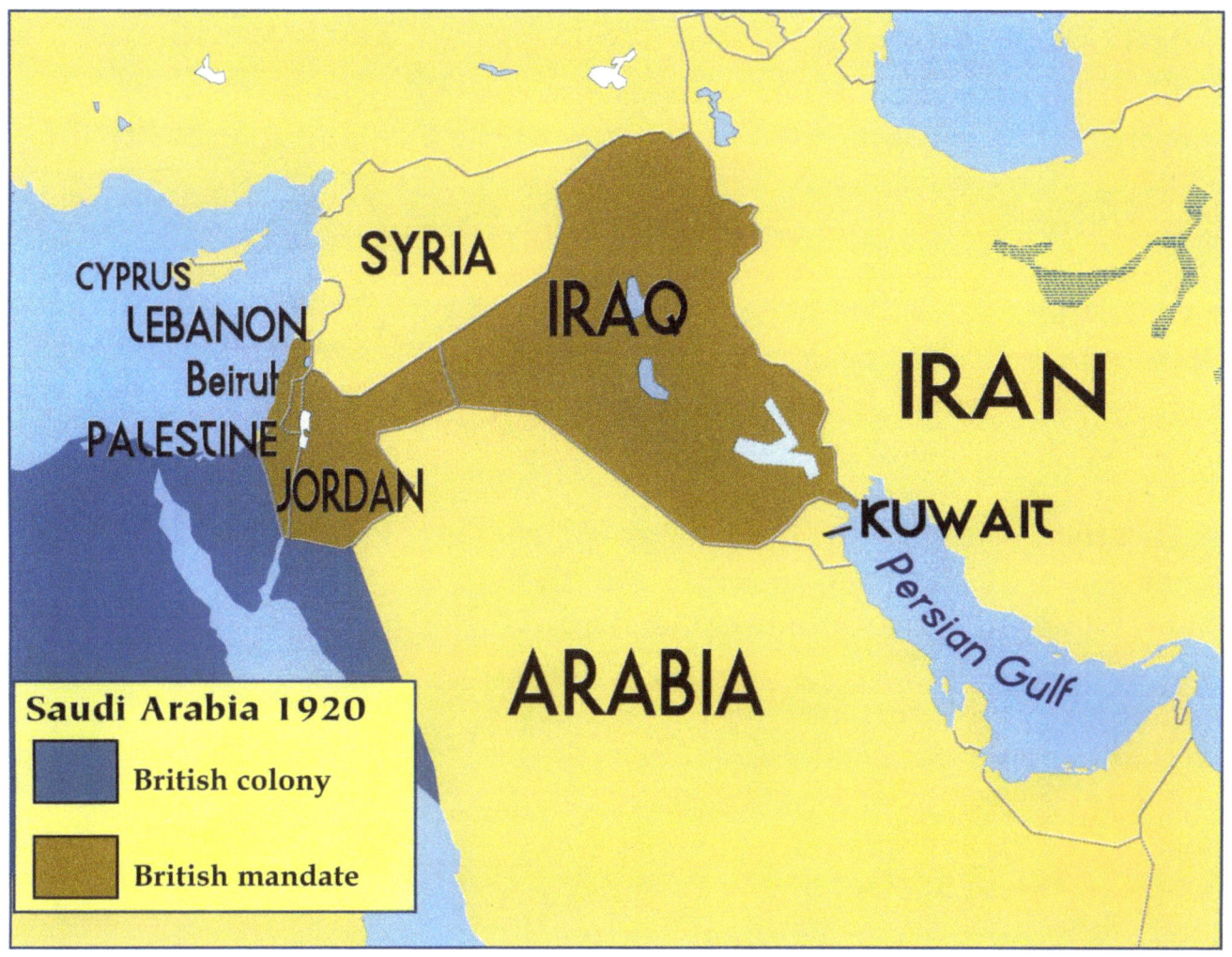

The map on this page, representing the united Kingdom of Saudi Arabia in 1920, shows its newly formed boundaries with Jordan, Iraq, and Kuwait. As recently as 2002, the U.S. Central Intelligence Agency has indicated that portions of the southern and eastern Saudi border are still undetermined because details of the 1974 and 1977 treaties about specific boundaries with the Republic of Yemen and the United Arab Emirates have not been made public.

In 1932, Abd al-Aziz united Al Hasa, the remainder of the Najd, and the Hijaz as the Kingdom of Saudi Arabia. Revised boundaries with Jordan, Iraq, and Kuwait were established by a series of treaties negotiated in the 1920s. As a result, two neutral zones were created: one with Iraq and the other with Kuwait. The Saudi-Kuwaiti border, however, was not defined until 1983, and the boundaries between Saudi Arabia and the United Arab Emirates were not official until 1974. Saudi Arabia's southern boundary with the present-day Republic of Yemen was partially outlined by a treaty that ended a war between the two nations in 1932.

Border Disputes

Following that bloody war, the newly established Kingdom of Saudi Arabia signed a peace treaty with the present-day Republic of Yemen. This agreement, called the Treaty of Taif, determined their common border, but it would continue to be disputed for years to come. The reasons for this dispute were related to arguments over which country owned certain islands in the Red Sea.

Another section of the border with Yemen was determined in 1934, but the Saudi border running southeast from Najran was still unclear. This boundary became important in the 1990s after oil was discovered in the area. Saudi Arabia, interested in maintaining profits from its oil monopoly, objected to the exploration by foreign companies on behalf of the Republic of Yemen.

On May 1, 1998, Yemeni troops occupied an island in the Red Sea and fired upon Saudi border guards there. Afterward, each side claimed that the other's military had crossed the disputed border and attacked island villages. By July, Yemen claimed its forces had taken over Duwaima Island.

Both nations eventually reached an agreement. Saudi Arabia, represented by

Saudi Arabia, as seen in this current map, is a desert nation of thirteen provinces that is roughly one-fifth the size of the United States. Its population of 23,500,300 are Muslims who are governed according to Islamic law. Known as the world's largest oil-producing nation, Saudi Arabia continually battles with an unstable economy based primarily on the changing prices of oil across the globe. With less than two percent of its land suitable for agriculture, and a dwindling freshwater supply, in 2002 the Saudi government found itself forced to deal with its growing population while providing enough water and food for its people.

foreign minister Saud al-Faisal, and the Republic of Yemen, represented by Prime Minister Abdulkarim al Iryani, signed a border treaty in Jeddah on June 12, 2000, that established permanent land and sea borders.

Promising Resources

In 1936, the American-owned Arabian Standard Oil Company discovered oil in Dhahran, and the first commercial shipments were exported in September 1938. The Kuwait Oil Company, a joint Anglo-American enterprise, began production in 1946. Thereafter, oil was discovered throughout the Persian Gulf. Vast petroleum revenues brought enormous changes to Saudi Arabia and transformed the gulf states. The market for labor brought migrant workers from Yemen, India, Pakistan, and the Philippines.

Abd al-Aziz II died in 1953 and was succeeded by his oldest son,

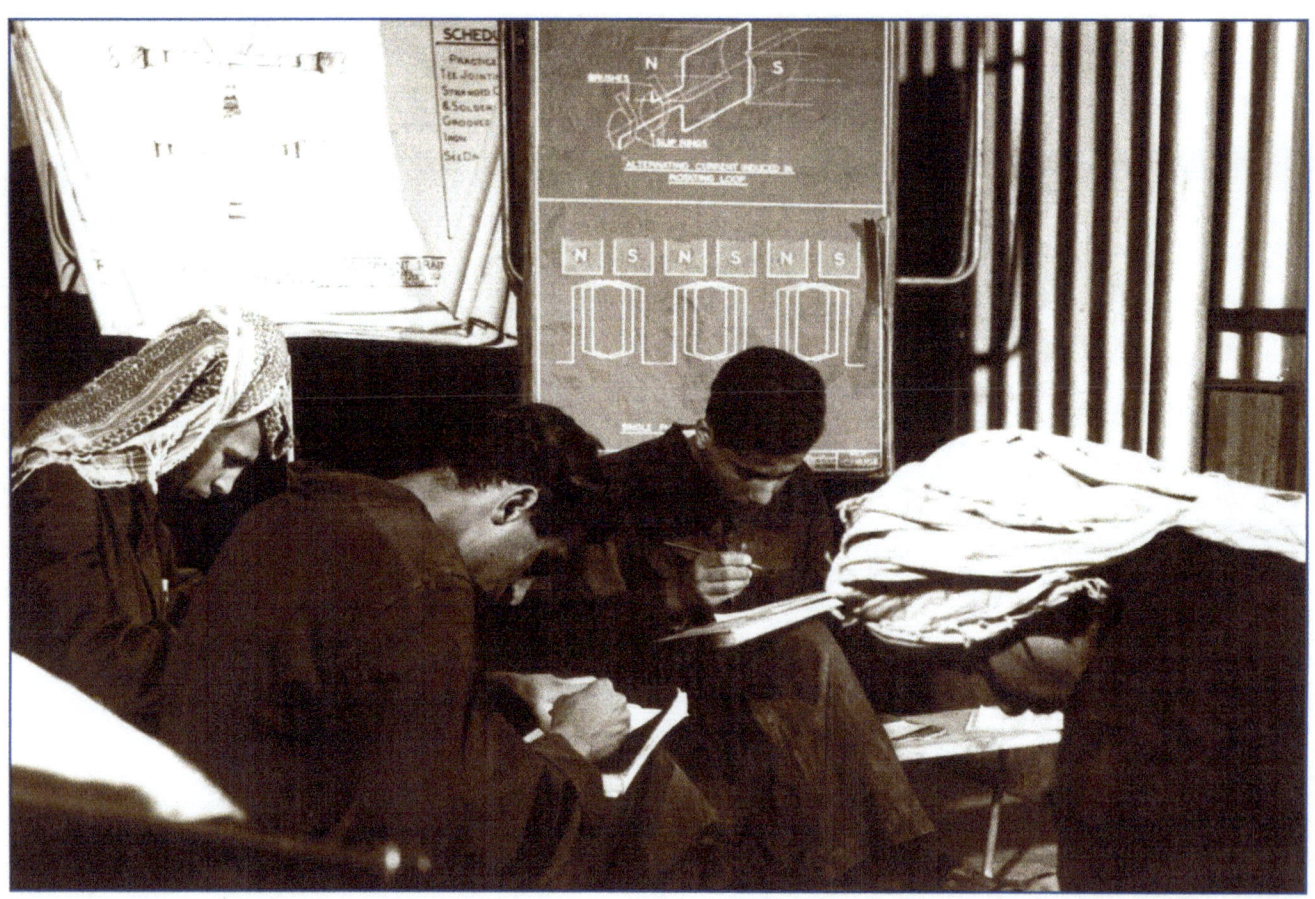

This photograph, taken in Kuwait in 1952, shows the teaching staff of one of the Kuwait Oil Company's training schools. The students are learning the principles of basic electrical maintenance. Their day was equally divided between academic study and vocational hands-on training.

Saud, who reigned for eleven years. In 1964, Saud abdicated in favor of his half brother, Faisal, who had served as foreign minister. Proclaimed king in 1964 by royal family members and religious leaders, Faisal also served as prime minister.

In 1975, Faisal was assassinated by a nephew, who was later executed. Faisal was succeeded as king and prime minister by his half brother Khalid; another half brother, Prince Fahd, was named crown prince and first deputy prime minister. King Khalid gave Crown Prince Fahd the power to oversee international and domestic affairs.

In 1982, Khalid died, and Fahd became king and prime minister. Another half brother, Abdullah, was named crown prince and first deputy prime minister. Under King Fahd, the Saudi economy adjusted to sharply lower oil revenues resulting from declining global oil prices. Saudi Arabia supported neutral shipping in the gulf during periods of the Iran-Iraq War (1980–1988) and aided Iraq's war-strained economy. King Fahd played a major part in bringing about the cease-fire between Iraq and Iran.

In the early 1990s, King Fahd played a key role before and during the Persian Gulf War (1990–1991).

United States president George W. Bush greets Saudi Arabia's crown prince Abdullah on Bush's 1,600-acre ranch on April 25, 2002, in Crawford, Texas. President Bush and Crown Prince Abdullah discussed the Israeli-Palestinian conflict during a bilateral meeting and luncheon.

Fahd consolidated the coalition forces against Iraq and helped free Kuwait. Acting as a personal spokesman for the coalition, Fahd helped bridge Western and Arab countries, as well as other outside nations. He urged other Islamic countries to join the coalition.

King Fahd suffered a stroke in November 1995. Since 1997, Crown Prince Abdullah has taken on government responsibilities.

TIMELINE

5000 BC   Mesopotamia flourishes
3300 BC   Writing begins in Sumer
2500 BC   Egyptians build the Pyramids
2400 BC   Assyrian Empire is established
2334 BC   Rule of Sargon I
1750 BC   Rule of Hammurabi in Babylonia
638 BC   Approximate birth of Persian prophet Zoroaster (Zarathrustra)
600 BC   Cyrus the Great establishes the Achaemenid Empire
586 BC   Approximate birth of Buddha
331 BC   Alexander the Great captures Babylon
323 BC   Alexander the Great dies
AD 200   Sassanians rise to power
AD 226   Approximate date Zoroastrianism is established
AD 313   Christianity is accepted by the Romans
AD 570   Birth of Muhammad
AD 600   Roman, Parthian, and Kushan Empires flourish
AD 610   Muhammad's first revelation
AD 622   Buddhism begins its spread from India to Asia
AD 625   Muslims control Mesopotamia and Persia
AD 632   Death of Muhammad
AD 633–700   Followers of Islam spread their faith
AD 685   Shiite revolt in Iraq
AD 750   Abbasid caliphate, Iraq
AD 751   Arabs learn papermaking from the Chinese
AD 762   City of Baghdad is founded
AD 1215   Genghis Khan captures China and moves westward
AD 1220   Mongols sack Bukhara, Samarkand, and Tashkent
AD 1258   Mongols sack Baghdad
AD 1379   Timur invades Iraq
AD 1387   Timur conquers Persia
AD 1453   Ottoman Empire captures Constantinople and begins overtaking Asia
AD 1498   Vasco da Gama reaches India
AD 1526   Babur establishes Mughal Empire
AD 1534   Ottomans seize Iraq
AD 1554   First Russian invasion into central Asia
AD 1632   Taj Mahal is built
AD 1739   Nadir Shah invades the Mughal Empire, sacks Delhi
AD 1740   Ahmed Shah Durrani founds kingdom in Afghanistan
AD 1858   British rule is established in India
AD 1932   Saudi Arabia is founded by Abd al-Aziz ibn Sa'ud
AD 1947   India declares its independence; East/West Pakistan succession
AD 1975   Saudi king Faisal is assassinated
AD 1991   Saudi Arabia is involved in attacks on Iraq
AD 2001   Saudi king Fahd calls for an end to terrorism
AD 2002   The U.S. requests to use military facilities in Saudi Arabia to attack Iraq

GLOSSARY

Al-Sa'ud The House of Sa'ud; the descendants of Muhammad ibn Sa'ud.

bedouin An Arab of any of the nomadic tribes of the desert.

emir A commander. In Saudi Arabia, "amir" often means "prince," but it can also refer to the governor of a province.

exile To banish or expel from one's country or home.

fanaticism Uncritical outlook or devotion, usually associated with religious beliefs.

frankincense An aromatic gum resin obtained from African and Asian trees of the genus *Boswellia* and used chiefly as incense and in perfumes.

fundamentalism A movement or attitude stressing strict and literal adherence to a set of basic principles usually associated with religious beliefs.

Ikhwan The brotherhood of desert warriors founded by Abd al-Aziz II.

imam The leader of congregational prayers. Many Sunni Muslims use the word to mean the leader of the Islamic community. Among Shiite Muslims the word has several meanings, but when capitalized it indicates a descendant of the House of Ali.

monotheism The act of worshiping one god only. Islam, Christianity, and Judaism are monotheistic religions.

nomad A member of a group of people who have no fixed home and move according to the seasons from place to place in search of food, water, and grazing land for their animals.

oasis A fertile spot in a desert, made so by the presence of water.

peninsula A piece of land that projects into a body of water and is connected to the mainland.

polytheism The act of worshiping many gods.

Sharia Islamic law.

sharif A descendant of Muhammad through his daughter Fatima.

sheik A leader or chief. Applied either to political leaders of tribes or towns, or learned religious leaders.

Shiite A member of the smaller of the two sects of Islam. The Shiites supported the claims of Ali and his line to the leadership of the Muslim community.

Sunni The larger of the two sects of Islam. The Sunni, who rejected claims to Ali's line, believe that they are the true followers of the sunna, the guide to proper Muslim behavior set forth by Muhammad.

wadi A valley, gully, or streambed that remains dry except during the rainy season, when it fills with rain runoff.

Wahhabi or **Wahhabism** The name used outside Saudi Arabia to designate the official government interpretation of Islam in Saudi Arabia. The faith is a puritanical concept preached by Muhammad ibn 'Abd al-Wahhab.

FOR MORE INFORMATION

Royal Embassy of Saudi Arabia
Information Office
Washington, DC
(202) 337-4076
(202) 337-4134
Web site:
http://www.saudiembassy.net

Web Sites

Due to the changing nature of Internet links, the Rosen Publishing Group, Inc., has developed an online list of Web sites related to the subject of this book. This site is updated regularly. Please use this link to access the list:

http://www.rosenlinks.com/liha/saar/

FOR FURTHER READING

Anscombe, Frederick F. *The Ottoman Gulf: The Creation of Kuwait, Saudi Arabia, and Qatar*. New York: Columbia University Press, 1997.

Heinrichs, Ann. *Saudi Arabia*. New York: Grolier Publishing, 2001.

Honeyman, Susannah. *Saudi Arabia*. Austin, TX: Raintree/Steck-Vaughn Publishers, 1995.

Long, David E. *The Kingdom of Saudi Arabia*. Gainsville, FL: University Press of Florida, 1998.

McCarthy, Kevin M. *Saudi Arabia: A Desert Kingdom*. Parsippany, NJ: Dillon Press, 1997.

Vassilier, Alexei. *The History of Saudi Arabia*. New York: New York University Press, 2000.

BIBLIOGRAPHY

Central Intelligence Agency. "CIA—The World Factbook—Saudi Arabia." Retrieved May 2002 (http://www.cia.gov/cia/publications/factbook/geos/sa.html).

Foster, Lelia Merrell. *Enchantment of the World: Saudi Arabia*. Chicago: Children's Press, 1993.

Goodwin, William. *Saudi Arabia*. San Diego: Lucent Books, 2001.

Janin, Hunt. *Cultures of the World: Saudi Arabia*. Tarrytown, NY: Times Books/Marshall Cavendish, 1993.

Library of Congress. "Saudi Arabia—A Country Study." Retrieved May 2002 (http://lcweb2.loc.gov/frd/cs/satoc.html).

The Saudi Arabian Information Resource. Retrieved May 2002 (http://www.saudinf.com).

Vassiliev, Alexei. *The History of Saudi Arabia*. New York: University Press, 2000.

INDEX

A
Abd Allah, 42, 47–48, 50–51
Abd ar-Rahman, 51
Abdullah, 59
Abu Bakr, 34, 38
Abyssinians, 16, 17, 26
Al-Hirah tribe, 26–27
Ali, 35, 38, 39

B
bedouins (nomads), 5, 12, 13, 26, 27, 28, 32, 54
Byzantine Empire, 27–28

C
caliphs, 34, 35, 38, 41

E
Egypt, 7, 15, 19, 24, 36, 41, 46, 47–48, 50

F
Fahd, 59
Faisal, 59

G
Ghassanids, 26, 27, 28
Great Britain, 48, 51, 54

H
Hadramites, 17, 21, 22, 26
hajj (pilgrimage), 6, 11, 33, 36, 41
Hijaz, 10–11, 41, 46–47, 48, 50, 52, 54, 55
Himyarites, 18, 19, 24, 26, 28

I
Ikhwan, 54
Imru' al-Qays, 26–27
Iran, 27, 35, 44, 59
Iraq, 28, 35, 38, 44, 46, 48, 50, 52, 54, 55, 59
Islam, 6, 11, 16, 17, 28, 29, 32–35, 36–39, 41, 44, 46, 48, 52, 54, 59

K
Khadija, 32, 33
Khalid, 59
Kharijites, 38
Kindah, 26, 28

L
Lakhmids, 26–27, 28

M
Ma'rib, 18, 19, 20
Mecca, 6, 11, 16, 28, 29, 32, 33, 34, 36, 41, 46, 50, 54
Medina, 6, 11, 32, 35, 36, 41, 44, 46, 54
Minaeans, 17, 19, 21, 22, 28
Muawiyah, 38
Muhammad, 6, 17, 28, 29–34, 35, 36–38
Muhammad Ali, 47, 48

N
Nabataeans, 15, 28
Najd, 7–10, 41, 42, 44, 46, 47, 48, 50, 52, 55

O
oil, 5, 7, 10, 11, 52, 56, 58, 59
Ottomans, 46–47, 48, 50, 51, 52, 54

P
Persian Gulf War, 59
Persians, 16, 28, 35

Q
Qatabanians, 17, 19–21, 22, 26
Quraysh, 26, 28, 29, 33, 34

R
Rashid, Muhammad ibn, 50–51
Riyadh, 7, 10, 16, 42, 48, 51, 52
Romans, 16, 19, 22–24, 35

S
Sabaeans, 17–19, 20, 21, 22, 24, 26, 28
Sadr ad Din Agha Khan, 39
Saud, 58–59
Sa'ud, Abd al-Aziz I, 46, 47
Sa'ud, Abd al-Aziz II, 42, 50, 51, 52–54, 55, 58
Sa'ud, house of (Al-Sa'ud), 10, 38, 41, 42–46, 47, 48–51
Sa'ud, Muhammad ibn, 42, 46, 48
Saudi Arabia
  ancient history of, 13–16
  early tribes of, 17–21, 22, 24–28, 29
  economy of, 5, 10, 59
  founding of kingdom, 52, 54–56
  geography of, 5–6, 7–12, 16
  regions of, 7–12
  religion in, 6, 29, 33, 34–35, 39, 48–50, 54
  ruling family of, 6, 10, 41, 58–59
  society of, 6
Shiite Muslims, 38–39, 44, 46
Sunni Muslims, 39
Syria, 15, 19, 38, 46

T
trade/trade routes, 15–16, 17, 18, 19, 20, 21, 22–24, 26, 28, 29, 34
Treaty of Taif, 56
Turki ibn Abd Allah, 48

U
Umar ibn al-Khattab, 34, 38
Umayyad dynasty, 28, 35
Uthman, 28, 35, 38

W
Wahhab, Muhammad ibn 'Abd al-, 41, 42, 44–46, 54
Wahhabi/Wahhabism, 41, 44, 46–50, 51, 54

Y
Yemen, 7, 11, 20, 24, 26, 28, 55, 56–58

About the Author
Nancy L. Stair is an editor and author of several young adult books. She lives in New York City.

Acknowledgments
Special thanks to Aisha Khan for her generous insight into Middle Eastern and Asian history and culture.

Photo Credits
Cover (map), pp. 1 (foreground), 4–5, 52–53 © 2002 Geoatlas; cover (background), p. 1 (background) © Royalty-Free/Corbis; cover (top left), p. 50 © Hulton/Archive/Getty Images; cover (bottom left), p. 33 © AKG Photo; cover (bottom right), p. 35 © Victoria and Albert Museum, London/Art Resource, NY; p. 6 © Robin Laurance/Impact Photos; pp. 8–9 © The British Library; p. 10 © James David Worldwide; pp. 11, 18 (bottom), 59 © AFP/Corbis; p. 12 © NASA/Corbis; pp. 14–15, 22–23, 24–25, 27, 30–31, 36–37, 42–43, 44–45, 49, 55 maps designed by Tahara Hasan; p. 15 (inset) © Caroline Penn/Corbis; p. 18 (top) © Elio Ciol/Corbis; pp. 20–21 © Scala/Art Resource, NY; p. 32 © AKG London/Jean-Louis Nou; p. 34 © AKG London; p. 39 © Art Resource, NY; pp. 40–41 © Alinari/Art Resource, NY; pp. 47, 56–57 courtesy of The General Libraries, The University of Texas at Austin; p. 58 © Bettmann/Corbis.

Series Design and Layout
Tahara Hasan

Photo Research
Elizabeth Loving

www.ingramcontent.com/pod-product-compliance
Lightning Source LLC
Chambersburg PA
CBHW041116070526
44584CB00002B/185